NO ONE
SUCCEEDS
ALONE

NO ONE SUCCEEDS ALONE

LEARN EVERYTHING

YOU CAN

from

EVERYONE YOU CAN

ROBERT REFFKIN

Houghton Mifflin Harcourt

Boston   New York   2021

For information about permission to reproduce selections from
this book, write to trade.permissions@hmhco.com or to Permissions,
Houghton Mifflin Harcourt Publishing Company,
3 Park Avenue, 19th Floor, New York, New York 10016.

hmhbooks.com

Library of Congress Cataloging-in-Publication Data
Names: Reffkin, Robert, author.
Title: No one succeeds alone : learn everything you can from
everyone you can / Robert Reffkin.
Description: Boston : Houghton Mifflin Harcourt, 2021. | Includes index.
Identifiers: LCCN 2020039129 (print) | LCCN 2020039130 (ebook) |
ISBN 9780358454618 (hardback) | ISBN 9780358449812 | ISBN 9780358449881 |
ISBN 9780358440017 (ebook)
Subjects: LCSH: Reffkin, Robert. | Chief executive officers — Biography. |
Children of single parents — Biography. | Success in business.
Classification: LCC HC102.5.R429 A3 2021 (print) | LCC HC102.5.R429 (ebook) |
DDC 650.1 — dc23
LC record available at https://lccn.loc.gov/2020039129
LC ebook record available at https://lccn.loc.gov/2020039130

Book design by Greta D. Sibley

Printed in the United States of America
DOC 10 9 8 7 6 5 4 3 2 1

For Raia, Ruby, and River

CONTENTS

FOREWORD

When I first met Robert Reffkin, he was just starting Compass. I had already heard about his spark and passion from others I respected. He had a bold vision for reimagining the real estate industry by creating a technology platform to make the searching and selling experience seamless and intelligent for agents and their clients.

I could relate to that vision and his passion, and felt a kinship with Robert. More than two decades ago, I dreamed of reimagining the software business by making it as easy to purchase and use business applications as it is to buy a book on Amazon. The result was Salesforce, and today the company is the world's number one customer relationship management platform, with more than $20 billion in annual revenue.

Robert and I have followed a similar path in some ways. We were both entrepreneurs from an early age, earning enough in high school to help us pay for college. We both had mothers in our lives who encouraged us to pursue our passions even when they took surprising turns — my wanting to visit the UK as a fifteen-year-old to learn about castles for a video game I was building or Robert's needing to stay out past midnight several nights a week for his high school DJ business.

And as they did in my case, not many people understood why Robert would leave his comfortable perch at a well-established company for the high-risk start-up world. But Robert was able to prevail, and this book is a testament to his exceptional ability to transform adversity into energy that has propelled him forward throughout his life and work.

It's clear that Robert's approach to business comes from his unique life story and values. Growing up Black and Jewish in Berkeley, California, he was inspired by his single-parent mother, Ruth. He was able to see every obstacle and setback as an opportunity and a way to hone his particular strengths.

Robert possesses critical traits that every leader aspires to have — the ability to listen, empathize, and learn from others. Robert deeply understands that no one succeeds alone. He has sought out mentors throughout his life, and now, through this book, he can be a mentor to anyone who dreams big. And he is committed not just to doing well but also to doing good in the world through his personal actions and his company.

Whether it's his collaborative approach to innovation, his strategy for connecting with mentors, his unwavering focus on customer needs, his way of building a company culture anchored in a sense of belonging, his beginner's mind open to endless possibilities, or his boundless optimism and persistence, everyone can learn from the way Robert engages with the world with gratitude, passion, and humanity.

— Marc Benioff, Chair and CEO, Salesforce

INTRODUCTION

Here's the most common way of telling my story.

Robert Reffkin was raised by a single mother without much money.

He made more than $100,000 running his first business while still in high school, DJing bar mitzvahs, high school dances, and house parties.

He graduated from Columbia University in two and a half years.

He was the only student from his college class hired at the New York headquarters of the exclusive management consulting firm McKinsey & Company.

He then had a fast-paced career at Lazard, the White House, and Goldman Sachs.

He started a nonprofit at age twenty-nine to help kids who were the first in their families to attend college.

He ran fifty marathons — one in each US state — to raise $1 million for charity.

He founded his own tech start-up, Compass, which is now worth billions of dollars.

That's the heroic way to tell my story.

But it's nowhere near the *whole* story.

When my mom tucked me into bed at night when I was a child, she didn't tell me to have sweet dreams — she told me to have *big* dreams. And I always have. But it's not easy to turn big dreams into reality.

In my life, I've failed much more often than I've succeeded. The only reason I've accomplished *anything* is because I learned early how to bounce back with unrelenting energy and passion, and come up with a new dream every time I stumbled.

No matter how hard I tried to succeed in high school and college, I always ended up with a C average.

I failed to land literally hundreds of different college scholarships that I applied for.

I applied to dozens of jobs as I was graduating from college and was turned down by all of them except one.

I felt like an impostor in every job I had in my twenties, like I was one day away from being fired — and in many cases, I wasn't wrong.

I knew nothing about running a nonprofit when I launched New York Needs You, and our first year of trial and error was a lot more error than anything else.

Our first idea for Compass failed to make renting a home more efficient for our customers, so just one year in, we had to pivot and change the entire business model.

Much of the early team lost faith in my leadership because of that pivot, and I was almost forced out of my own company.

At Compass, we've experimented with hundreds of offerings

for our customers—software, support programs, and marketing. Most didn't work at all.

It's only because I've kept going—because I've been eager to learn from every challenge and keep trying until we solve each problem—that I'm here today. And because, from a very young age, I've never believed that the answers were inside me. I've always looked for answers in the work of others trying to do similar things, in the wisdom of my mentors, and in the energy of my collaborators.

I've learned that opportunity is everywhere around you if you're willing to dream, ask, and listen.

The lessons I've learned are grounded in the journey I've taken. So I'd like to share some of my story—and some of the lessons people have taught me—with you in the pages that follow.

My dreams for this book

Before someone at Compass embarks on a project, I ask them, "What does success look like?" as a way to focus their energy on the results that really matter. So I'll take my own advice and do the same.

Here's what success looks like for this book if all my dreams for it—and you—come true.

> *Something you read in this book will inspire you to dream bigger than you ever have before.*
> *Something in this book will help you realize your full potential—not just the potential you think you have right now.*
> *Something you read here will motivate you to reach out and help someone else make their dreams come true.*

And all these "somethings" added together will make this book valuable enough to you that you'll decide to give a copy to someone you know within three months of finishing it yourself.

If all that happens, it will mean that you have come to believe, as I do, that no one succeeds alone — and that together anything is possible.

Best,
Robert

FINDING MY PLACE IN THE WORLD

I've felt out of place my entire life.

My mother is an Israeli immigrant. My father was an African American man from Louisiana who left me and my mom when I was just a baby. Through his actions, my dad, in effect, told me that I did not belong.

After I was born, my mother's parents — my grandparents — asked her only one question.

They didn't ask, "Is he happy?"

They didn't ask, "Is he healthy?"

They asked, "What is he?"

My mom said, "He is Jewish . . . and Black."

My grandparents immediately hung up the phone and disowned us both. From that day to their death, I never met them. I never even spoke to them. They made it clear that I didn't belong.

From that point on, it was just the two of us trying to make it on our own.

When I was growing up, my mom made it clear that no matter what anyone else said or thought about us we always had each other. When I was with her, I belonged.

But as I got older, I began to notice all the ways that I didn't fit in and all the people who didn't accept me. The people who asked my mother if I was adopted while I was standing right there. The middle school teachers who blamed me for fights at school that I had nothing to do with. The high school administrators who came down hard on me and some other kids of color when we shared the ways that the school's curriculum made us feel unwelcome.

The more out of place I felt, the more I craved a genuine sense of belonging in the larger world.

That's why I moved to New York City—one of the most diverse cities in the world, a city where a biracial kid like me would have as good a shot as anybody at feeling at home and gaining a sense of belonging.

But as I became accustomed to New York, I realized that where I lived was only part of it. Yes, I had found my city, but I still felt like I needed to find my *place.*

After college, I tried management consulting, finance, government, education, and various romantic relationships. No matter what I did, though, something was still missing. I was always running, looking to the future for the feeling of belonging that kept eluding me in the present.

Your place in the world is sometimes an actual physical place: a home, a neighborhood, or a city. But it can also be something that speaks to your sense of purpose in life: a job, a community, a relationship. Your place is wherever you feel fulfilled, alive, and at peace.

For me, the answer turned out to be finding my personal mission in life (which I'll share more about later in the book) and a partner for life who accepted me completely: my wife, Benís.

I believe that to be your best self you have to be your *authentic* self.

And you can't be your authentic self until you find your place in the world.

The only Black kid at the synagogue
Adapt like water and you'll be unstoppable

I was the only Black kid in my synagogue — but when I was with the other Black kids from school, I didn't fit in easily either, since I was mixed *and* Jewish.

People didn't know what to do with me, how to talk to me, what to say to me.

My being different made many people uncomfortable — even when they were well-meaning.

Since there was no community that I belonged to without question, I was never able to let down my guard and just be me. I had to do the work of figuring out everyone else around me all the time, and I got very good at adapting myself to make other people comfortable. I had to learn, on my own, how to be comfortable being uncomfortable.

I learned to talk to White people and Black people.

Wall Street types and nonprofit types.

Kids whose parents had no idea how to play the game and kids whose parents practically invented the game.

I learned how to set different kinds of people at ease. I watched their faces closely when I spoke to them to see which things connected and which things did not — then repeated the things that clicked in other conversations.

I've had to study people with the kind of focus and care that other people study books with.

It's certainly not fair that some people can be themselves and others need to constantly present different parts of themselves in different situations in order to make others comfortable. When I was younger, I wished that *I* could be the one to be made comfortable sometimes rather than always doing that for others.

But I've made the personal choice not to focus on the unfairness. Instead of getting angry, I became determined to go further. I focused my energy on learning to adapt and adjust to more and more situations.

Being extremely adaptable is a hugely valuable skill.

It transforms every interaction into an *opportunity.*

These days, I might talk to an investor in Asia, a software engineer in Seattle, a newly hired real estate agent in Miami, my eldest daughter Raia on FaceTime, a junior marketing designer in New York, and a reporter from the *Wall Street Journal* — all in a single hour. And for each conversation, I adapt.

People throughout my life have made me feel like I don't belong. But I haven't listened. Being able to adapt to anything made me feel that I was never out of place and that no one could ever "put me in my place."

A mentor once said that I was like water: no matter what you set in its way, water finds a way to keep moving. It changes form, it tunnels deeply, it discovers a path around whatever obstacle it comes across on its journey. And slowly but surely, water wears away the obstacles that try to contain it, carving new paths that are easier to follow in the future.

I don't blame my father for what he did, but I do blame his ego

Don't underestimate the damage that ego can do

You might think that I learned about the dangers of selfish, hypercompetitive behavior by running up against some massive egos from high-flying executives in $5,000 suits in New York and Washington, DC. After all, I worked on Wall Street with investment bankers and alongside powerful politicians in the White House.

But I actually learned about the dangers of ego on the other side of the country as the child of an absent, abusive father who suffered from a heroin addiction. Not exactly the picture of a high-ego individual.

What I saw was that your ego can crush you as easily as it allows you to trample others.

I believe that my dad, like many men, collapsed under the pressure he felt to be "The Man." He moved from Louisiana to the Bay Area to follow his dreams of becoming a musician in the late 1960s. The fact that he didn't become the next Jimi Hendrix or John Coltrane was a massive blow to his sense of self. The racism that he experienced in his new city ground him down in ways big and small. The guilt and shame that came from not being able to support himself or his family financially was psychologically debilitating.

If he'd accepted himself and his own strengths and weaknesses, and had been a loving partner to my mom and a good dad to me, we would have never looked down on him for a second. We would have been so happy to have him in our lives. I would have been so happy to have a dad.

But his ego blinded him to our love. When he looked at us, he only saw us looking back at him—and he imagined that we didn't like what we saw. That's the terrible trick ego plays on you: making you become obsessed with what others think about *you* rather than what you can do for others.

The weight of my father's ego—and his disappointments—made him turn to drugs.

The weight of his ego—and the addictive power of drugs—led him to cheat, steal, and make risky decisions that eventually resulted in his contracting AIDS. At his worst, he would hit my mom and put both of us in danger. So much so that my mom had to move to a new city to escape his violence.

I feel so blessed to have been too young to remember my dad in this way. In a way, his abandoning me when he did is actually the greatest gift he gave me. While my mom quietly wrestled with serious emotional trauma, I was able to have a happy childhood.

He's been gone now for a long time. My mother and I have forgiven him for everything he did, but we haven't forgotten. We learned from our experiences and our memories of him.

Children everywhere look to their moms and dads to understand what to do and how to be a person. I've learned what *not* to do and how *not* to be from my dad. They've been painful lessons, but they've also probably been more instructive because of that. Pain can be a powerful teacher.

Seeing the ways my dad's life fell apart taught me how to hold my life together. I saw my father give up on his life, and it gave me the determination to never do the same. Because of him, I'll always keep trying, keep striving, keep showing up.

While ego can sometimes give you a boost of energy or a drive to succeed, I think it can often be more dangerous than it's worth.

It's wiser to focus on collaboration over competition.

To care more about doing good than making yourself look good.

To give credit freely rather than seeking glory yourself.

To accept that you're a flawed person—like everyone is—with great strengths and real weaknesses.

To seek feedback so you can get better and better over time.

To be comfortable being your authentic self.

To be happy with who you are at the core.

If my dad had cared about any of that as much as he had cared about his own image, my life would not have been the same—and he'd probably be alive today.

The teacher who believed in me, the one who didn't, and the woman who had my back

Believing in people changes their lives

When I entered middle school as a sixth grader, my teacher sized me up and didn't like what she saw. Without any real evidence or cause, she decided that I should be taken out of her classroom and sent to the auxiliary trailers that had been installed near the playground for kids designated as needing special education.

Maybe the fact that I had brown skin and a lot of energy had absolutely nothing to do with it. Maybe I'd just had a bad day on my first day of school and she'd settled on a terrible first impression of me that she hadn't shaken.

But I worry that if, as an eleven-year-old Black male, I had been sent to those trailers, I never would have come back. I was standing at the opening of the infamous "school-to-prison pipeline," and my life may never have been the same if I'd gone down that path.

The most remarkable thing is that my *fifth* grade teacher had loved me.

Her name was Ms. Julie Blank, and we've become Facebook friends in recent years, so I reached out to her to ask what she remembered about me as a child. She recalled how much I respected my mom and how I would call out other kids if they told a joke at someone's expense. She described me as "just a very sweet kid. A good mixture of being calm and cheerful, usually on an even keel. Sharp. Hardworking."

I was just a kid, so I'm sure I also had bad days in her class when I was laughing when I should have been listening or when I was not picking up on some lesson quickly enough.

But Ms. Blank had seen me as a whole person.

And she had held on to her image of me at my best.

She was the sort of person who went through life believing in other people's potential. I've realized that this is a choice you can make in life — and it's a choice with profound consequences.

Ms. Blank, who has now been a schoolteacher for nearly four decades, believes that her students will achieve whatever you expect them to. If she expects everyone to be on time and focused, they will be. If she expects everyone to be rowdy and disrespectful, they will be. If she calls on girls less than boys, they'll get the message and expect less of themselves, too.

She told me that the key to ensuring that this philosophy works is making the kids believe that you truly believe in them. "If you love them sincerely and you make clear what you expect, it will happen," she told me.

When I told her recently that my sixth grade teacher had tried to track me into special education, she was stunned — and angry. "Even thirty years later, I'm feeling my mama bear come out. I pity the fool who underestimates Robert Reffkin."

I was lucky that my mom was also the sort of person who believed in other people's potential — especially her own son's. (She may have something in common with all other mothers on that one.)

When she heard about my teacher's plan to track me into the special education trailers, she marched to school to meet with her in person — and inform her that under no circumstances would that be happening. My mom is able to marshal a lot of intensity when my future is on the line (something else she may share with a lot of other mothers), and as a highly educated White woman, she was listened to a lot more than a young Black child.

After weeks of advocacy from my mom, my sixth grade teacher gave me another chance to prove myself, which I was able to do without much difficulty. For months afterward, my mom kept pushing the teachers, administrators, and others at the school to make significant changes in how they treated students like me — but she ended up disappointed by their indifference and intransigence. The next year, she found another school for me where I was less likely to be underestimated.

I still think about the other kids who were assigned to those trailers. Many of them probably hadn't had a teacher like Ms. Blank to believe in them or a mom like mine who could fight for them and be listened to by the people in charge.

I've never forgotten that lesson. When I have to choose whether to believe the best or the worst about someone, I choose to believe the best. I try to see greatness in everyone around me, and like Ms. Blank, I aspire to be the kind of person who can help them realize their unlimited potential.

The barber who changed my life

If you seek opportunity, you'll see it everywhere

When you get dressed up to go on a first date, you know it's an opportunity. When you show up for your first day at a new job, you know it's an opportunity. When you decide to record your parents' old stories for posterity, you know it's an opportunity.

But the truth is: every time you leave your house is an opportunity. Every time you talk with another human being is an opportunity. Whether you're having a one-on-one meeting with your manager, making small talk with someone in line at the grocery store, or shooting someone a quick email — those are all opportunities.

Every interaction, every conversation, every moment is an *opportunity.*

The only question is: Are you proactively seeking opportunity? Are your eyes, ears, and heart open to all the possibility around you?

When I was twelve years old, I was getting a haircut at the barber's. The woman who was cutting my hair had a lot of energy and had a real '80s vibe to her. She was chatty and she wanted to talk, so we were talking. I could have tuned her out. I could have ignored her. I could have gone through the motions without really listening. I was just a kid after all.

But as she was chewing her gum and cutting my hair, she mentioned how the kid of someone she knew had gotten into a better private school with the help of a nonprofit program.

That got my attention. I'd had a terrible year in sixth grade, a time when kids start caring about popularity and trying to be cool (which mostly meant being mean) and everyone becomes suddenly very conscious of race. Teachers began to single me

out, and classmates I'd known for years turned into bullies overnight.

I was now a seventh grader in my first year at a new middle
school, and it was going a lot better. But it was still difficult in a
lot of ways, and I was looking forward to finding a high school
that was an even better fit for me.

So I asked the barber how that kid had gotten in. She told me
about a nonprofit organization called A Better Chance. The way
she said it — "Yeah, I've got a friend and A Better Chance helped
them, I think" — would have made it very easy to ignore her or
forget what she said. But I didn't. I recognized this as an opportunity, and I grabbed it.

I told my mom about A Better Chance, and we figured out
how to get in touch with them. They helped me apply to all the
best schools in Oakland and San Francisco with a single free application. They helped us dream much bigger about what might
be possible and what might be worth it. For example, we could
have ruled out schools that required a two-hour commute each
morning, but we didn't. We focused on what would be best — and
only after we'd learned more about that did we shift to figuring
out how to make it possible.

In the end, I directly credit A Better Chance for helping me
get into what was considered one of the best high schools in San
Francisco. But I'm even more grateful to the barber who told me
about A Better Chance in the first place, and to my mother, who
raised me to always be on the lookout for opportunities.

My mindset didn't create opportunities that didn't exist. But
it *did* help me notice all the opportunities around me. Through
my experiences with A Better Chance and the other nonprofits
that supported me, I developed the view that there are often more
people who want to help you than you have time to accept help

from. There are also people who *don't* want to help you, and you may come across people who are rooting against you. But if you focus your attention on spotting and connecting with those who do want to help, you'll likely never run out of opportunity.

The big plan I made at age thirteen
Dream out your future on paper — then tear the paper up

When I was thirteen, I took a huge sheet of paper and charted out the courses I would take when I got to high school. I thought about all the knowledge I'd gain and all the skills I'd learn — US History, AP Biology, AP Calculus, AP Chemistry — and all the dreams that those courses would make possible.

That day, before I even *started* high school, I actually felt like I'd already finished it.

Physically seeing the plan in front of me and imagining every step of the journey, I was able to transport myself to my final destination. As I wrote out the name of each class, I visualized myself sitting in each classroom and taking in all that information. As my plan progressed from semester to semester, I felt like I was making progress that quickly, too, racing toward my future. By the time I was done, I could almost *feel* the graduation gown on my back.

When I turned the fuzzy dreams in my head into very concrete dreams on the page, I felt a burst of energy that made it possible for me to chase those dreams in real life.

Energy is everything. There's a much bigger difference between doing something and *not* doing something than there is between the ways you might go about doing it. Going from zero to one is what matters. And by definition, you can't do anything without energy.

Yet generating energy is something most people don't take seriously or even think about. If you don't know what fires you up and gets you going, you'll never be able to reach your full potential. Just imagine trying to drive a car without realizing you needed to fill up its gas tank (or charge its battery).

I sketched out my future on the same type of enormous paper when I was accepted into Columbia.

And when I started New York Needs You.

And when I started to seriously think about running fifty marathons.

And when I founded Compass.

I've even done it at the lowest moments in my life, like after I had my heart broken by my college sweetheart in my early twenties or after I lost my entire life savings in the stock market.

After both situations, I got some paper the next morning and sketched out massive multiyear plans to earn back the love and the money I'd lost.

Does that mean I followed *all* of those plans to the letter? Not at all. During high school, I took at most a third of the classes I sketched out on that paper when I was a young teenager. But I know that I was more successful, more passionate, and more inspired by my high school experience because I poured so much possibility into it before I even started.

By writing out a plan, I'd created a vision for my high school experience. A vision that I could hold true to even if I didn't follow the specific steps on the path — and to be clear, I never followed the exact steps of *any* plan from start to finish, in my life.

As it turned out, the overall vision mattered more than the plan. The vision is what gave me energy. But I did need the plan to make the vision come into focus and make my dreams real enough to start pursuing them.

THE FIVE-STEP PROCESS FOR SUCCESS

Looking back at my life, I've followed the same pattern over and over.

I dream up a big idea, a big goal, or a big vision. Something huge, ambitious, and worth pursuing.

I sketch out the future of that idea on paper in a way that energizes me.

I try out the idea in a way that lets me get real feedback from real people, sometimes by asking a potential customer if the product or service sounds useful to them, sometimes by actually building a demo version of whatever it is and asking someone to use it and share their reactions.

It succeeds or fails — or more often, it does a little of both. But it almost never leads me to the sketched-out future or my big dream.

I reflect on those results: what worked, what didn't, why that might have been, and how I can resolve those issues. Then I dream up a new dream informed by what I just learned, and the process begins again.

It's simple.

1. Dream big
2. Sketch out the future
3. Try
4. Learn from your failures and successes
5. Dream up a new dream

Then repeat this simple process — forever.

What my first business taught me about myself

Help people you know be successful at something — anything —
as early in their lives as possible

I believe that the right dream for you is the one that gives you the most energy. But until you've done something in the world that you're proud of, it can be hard to discover that energy in yourself in the first place.

I was a pretty happy and friendly kid when I was young. But as life got harder for me in middle school, I sometimes felt like I was losing my way. I had trouble with some of my teachers for the first time. I changed schools. Some friends drifted away, and other friends turned their backs on me. All of a sudden, the White kids and the Black kids stopped hanging out together as much. Everyone became obsessed with being cool and popular. I started dreading going to school each morning.

I didn't feel like I got my bearings until I started my first successful little business during my freshman year of high school.

The business was simple: I would buy Rasta shirts, Rasta hats, essential oils, and puka-shell necklaces in bulk then sell them while commuting to and from high school.

Selling Rasta gear wasn't nearly as big or as life-changing as the DJ business I started soon after, but it was the beginning. I got my first real taste of accomplishment, financial independence, and purpose. Hawking those Bob Marley shirts and those green-yellow-red-and-black knit hats gave me a reason to reach out to people and start conversations. Selling the oils meant that girls had a reason to come over and talk to me. And the business helped me earn enough money to be able to buy things on my own without having to ask my mom.

The first lesson I learned from that business is that I liked working with other people much more than working alone. My best friend, Jabali, another biracial kid who felt out of place in our school, was the one who first got me into Rasta stuff (including the dreads I started growing around the same time). Before buying anything in bulk, I would always ask Jabali what he thought. Planning the business together made the business more successful and strengthened our friendship.

I also learned that the risk of rejection was worth it in order to achieve the rush of satisfaction that came from every sale. At first it was scary to speak up and try to sell the items on a crowded bus or BART train. But it soon became natural — even fun. Every time someone bought something, I felt like I was making progress and getting better and that the future was going to be just a little brighter.

But the most important lesson was the simplest: if I try something, it might just work. If I hadn't learned that lesson then, I don't think I would have known myself well enough to chart the right path for my future.

There are too many people in our world who feel stuck, aimless, incapable. In many cases, all that stands between them and a better life is that first simple success — and the personal lessons that emerge from it. The achievement can be anything. Maybe it's selling your first handmade thing on Etsy. Maybe it's completing an online course in computer programming. Maybe it's running a mile two minutes faster than you did before.

What matters is that it leads to a sense of pride — and self-discovery.

How I made $100,000 DJing bar mitzvahs and high school parties
Love your customers more than your ideas

I discovered my first significant business opportunity while I was a student participating in a program run by the National Foundation for Teaching Entrepreneurship (now known as the Network for Teaching Entrepreneurship). At the end of the course, they hosted a business-plan competition judged by MBA students at UC Berkeley and several venture capitalists.

Having been to a number of parties for school as well as bar and bat mitzvahs, I noticed that they always had professional DJs — and I thought I could be just as good as they were. So I interviewed several DJs for research, wrote up a business plan, and was lucky enough to win. With the $500 award, a small loan from my mother, and my savings, I bought all the necessary equipment and got to work.

I wasn't the most skilled DJ. I didn't know or own more music than the other DJs. And I didn't have the loudest speakers or the best turntables. But I built a great business, which I called Rude Boy Productions.

My competitive advantage was that, unlike most DJs who played the music they liked, I would play whatever the guests wanted. I'd read the room and choose tracks that got people moving. Whenever I felt the energy start to fade, I'd switch it up quickly and get things pumping again.

I listened to my customers. I didn't let my pride and my personal preferences get in the way of what the crowd wanted. Focusing on the customer was the difference between playing to a packed house or an empty dance floor.

And to make sure the person who hired me was happy at the end of the night, I pledged to play up to twenty songs they requested (as long as they told me in advance so I could buy the songs if I didn't have them). I even promised them their money back if I didn't play all their picks. I called it the Rude Boy Productions guarantee.

I ended up being the most utilized DJ in the Bay Area private high school system for two years in a row. The more parties I worked, the more different songs I tried, the more crowds I figured out how to read — the more my business grew.

I made more money than I ever could have dreamed of while DJing in high school — enough to buy all the clothes and shoes I wanted, and help pay for college as well.

I worked hard — but that's not why I succeeded. I succeeded by listening to my customers, caring about them, and prioritizing their happiness over my own musical taste even as I became a moderately cool high schooler and they remained newly bar-mitzvahed middle schoolers.

The secret is to know that *you* don't know the secret — but your clients and customers *do*.

Why losing out on a $26 million inheritance hurt less than getting my jacket stolen

Four ways to avoid holding a grudge

My maternal grandparents taught me by their singular example how toxic it can be to hold a grudge. They refused to meet me their entire lives simply because my father was Black. When they died, my grandparents left a $26 million inheritance to my mother's only sister and left my mom a mere $100 — just enough to ensure that she couldn't contest the will.

But I think my grandparents lost out on more than we did. They were not happy people. When you hold on to resentments, they end up taking hold of you. They eat at you until the negativity consumes you. Meanwhile, my mom and I are surrounded by people we love and people who love us. We're happy. Our lives are full.

Holding a grudge does literally nothing for you — except hold you back.

So when people do me wrong in some way, I try to bounce back rather than dig in. It's not always easy, but it almost always works. Here's how I do it.

First: I try to let the affront go. In my experience, the vast majority of perceived slights, insults, or unfair dealings are simply misunderstandings. Even if it *was* intentional, I do my best to ignore it. I move forward in my life by willing myself to actually *forget* bad things that happen.

Second: if assuming good intentions doesn't work, I try empathy. I imagine the personal battles that other people are fighting, most of which I know nothing about. I try to picture how the situation may have looked from the other person's point of view.

For example, I don't hold a grudge against my dad for abandoning me. I can't be mad at someone battling addiction. And I know it wasn't easy to be a Black man with big dreams that he'd failed to realize in San Francisco almost fifty years ago.

Third: I use it as a learning experience to help me see people for who they are. There are lots of things in life that only hardship can teach you. For me, one of the toughest lessons has been that not everyone can be trusted.

I believe that the vast majority of people are good the vast majority of the time. But when I think about a huge number of people over the course of a lifetime, I know that at least a few of them will treat me poorly. Some people will lie to me. Others will lie about me. Of the thousands of people I deal with in business, a handful of folks will try to take advantage of me for their own financial gain.

By not letting this shock me, I can remove much of its negative power — and allow myself to focus on improving my intuition for the next time. Since I don't always see these people coming, I try to take notice and make a significant change in how I deal with them when they first show me their true colors. And while being a bit more guarded makes me sad sometimes, I've learned that it's the best way to protect all the good in my life.

Fourth: I try to harness the power of motivation. I hold no grudge against the critics and reporters who have predicted Compass's imminent failure over the years. I understand that it's their job to be skeptical. But rather than let their negative energy get me down, I transform it into a burst of positive energy that propels me forward.

Despite all these approaches, I am not able to let something go sometimes. Like everyone else in the world, I do carry some resentments. When all else fails, I simply allow myself to be okay with carrying a grudge as long as I can carry it lightly.

In high school, one of my good friends stole from me. He was such a good friend that he would sometimes come hang in my room even when I wasn't there yet. One day, I noticed one of my jackets had gone missing, and soon after, I saw him wearing my jacket on the playground. When I confronted him, he lied to my face. The lie and betrayal cut so much deeper than the theft that I've never been able to forgive him.

In cases like that, I try to accept that the hurt was just too painful to ignore or forget. Instead, I choose to forgive *myself* for not being able to let it go. *This is life,* I tell myself. These things will happen. You have to move forward. When I get comfortable carrying something negative with me, it loses much of its toxicity. More than the anger itself, it's often my frustration with being angry that weighs me down. If I can get rid of the frustration, it helps a lot.

Next time you're faced with a situation that's hard to get past, consider trying these approaches instead of holding a grudge.

1. Assume it was a misunderstanding
2. Empathize with the other person
3. Use the experience to learn about people
4. Harness it for motivation

And if you can't let it go, disarm it through empathy, transform it into a lesson or energy, or try to carry it as lightly as you can.

The college counselor who told me not to apply to my dream school

Don't just ignore the haters — turn their negativity into energy

During high school, I wasn't always sure I even wanted to go to college. My music business was booming and I was considering becoming a full-time DJ after graduation. But then I took a college-tour trip to New York with my mom and unexpectedly fell in love with Columbia University because of the beautiful campus, the energy of the city, and the admissions officer who made me feel like I would fit in and belong there.

His name was Peter Johnson. He got my attention by telling me that he'd had dreadlocks when he was younger, and he piqued my interest in the school by telling me that Lauryn Hill was a student there. I gave him my yellow Rude Boy Productions business card so he'd remember me as well as I remembered him. But this story is not about him.

When I got back to Berkeley, I set up a meeting with my high school guidance counselor to talk about my options. His advice was stark and right to the point: "Don't even apply. You don't have the grades to get in. It wouldn't be worth your time and money on the application fee."

In that moment, my desire to go to Columbia went from strong to absolute.

If someone tells me something is wonderful, I'll probably want to pursue it. If someone tells me I can't do something that's wonderful, I will stop at nothing to prove that person wrong.

To be fair, my guidance counselor was correct that with a C average I was certainly a long-shot candidate. But he was dead wrong that it wasn't worth trying. I have always believed that anything is possible and that, like someone in an intricate maze, you have to keep pressing ahead to find a way to your goal. It might not be easy and your success might not be probable, but it's always *possible*. Too many people give up because their goals aren't probable. As Wayne Gretzky said, "You miss 100 percent of the shots you don't take."

So in the months that followed, I obsessed about every tiny opportunity to improve my chances of being accepted. I tried to find every possible way to convince Columbia that they should accept me.

First, I mailed a personal, handwritten letter to the admissions officer to thank him for taking the time to talk to me, and I included my promotional DJ materials as well as a summary of all of my extracurricular activities.

When another Columbia admissions officer visited my high

school to speak to prospective applicants, I didn't just attend — I stayed after to talk to her personally, ask questions, and share my story. I walked her out of the building to her car and sent her a handwritten note the next day thanking her for her advice.

I decided to apply "early decision" to convey my passion and commitment.

I crafted my application essay to not only help them get to know me but also to justify and contextualize the weakest part of my application: my C average.

I studied harder for the SAT than I'd ever studied before, knowing that I needed to prove that I wasn't just hardworking and likable but also actually smart (at least in the ways that tests like that measure) — and it paid off.

You'll meet many skeptics and doubters who say they wish you well but still want you to know how likely it is that you'll ultimately fail. You'll meet cynics whose negative mindsets say that trying isn't worth it. You'll meet outright haters who love nothing more than watching you stumble or struggle or fall. And if you're trying to do big things, you'll find even more of those folks.

I don't really blame skeptics, doubters, cynics, and haters for being who they are. I don't expect them to ever change. And I know there's no way to completely avoid them.

The question I ask myself is: How can I transform all of their negativity into fuel for my own success? Like those movie heroes who visualize their ancestors when they need to summon their inner strength, I find myself visualizing all of the people who ever told me I can't do something when I need to take on a big challenge.

I want to acknowledge, though, that if you're from an underrepresented community and you have big dreams you're going to encounter even more doubters along your journey. There's nothing fair about having to work harder to prove the world wrong, and I get it when people feel that the deck is so stacked against them that it's not even worth trying.

Let me be clear, though. I don't think people should turn pain into positive energy because it's the *right* thing to do — I think people should turn pain into positive energy because it's the *most effective* way to realize your dreams.

How the difficulties of my childhood helped me open the door to my future

Turn your story into a beautiful narrative that inspires others

We all have a story to tell about ourselves and our lives — and there is a story that the world is likely to tell about us if we don't step up and tell it first.

Think about Steve Jobs. You could think of his story as "unpleasant college dropout forces his opinions on the world" or as the story that most of us are familiar with: "passionate visionary uses his obsessions with design and technology to transform billions of lives."

When I was a senior in high school, you could have told quite different stories about me depending on your vantage point.

Seventeen-year-old entrepreneur with big dreams and lots of potential juggles schoolwork and a fast-growing business all while helping out his single mother.

Dreadlocked Black DJ gets Cs in high school.

The first story might convince people to care about me and invest in me. The second story doesn't have a happy ending — at least not in the minds of most people.

Both stories were true. But the story I told would change

how the world saw me and treated me — and it had the power to change the course of my life.

I put more effort into my college application essay than any other piece of writing except this book. (I've included the entire essay here and resisted the temptation to edit it or update it now that I'm no longer a teenager.)

But I didn't stop with just that essay because I didn't want to rely on words alone to tell my story. I wanted my story to fit into a larger narrative.

When I'd first met Peter Johnson, the admissions officer, I'd made sure to tell him about the entrepreneurial lessons I was learning through my DJ business so he could start to understand me as a full person. I kept in touch throughout my application process. When I was in the local news for DJing a festival and when I was invited to a model United Nations conference, I sent him the news clippings.

Years later, after I'd been accepted to Columbia, graduated, and had worked for a few years, I was working late in the Lazard office on a Sunday evening, and I decided to reach out to Peter Johnson again. In my email, I wrote: "Thank you for taking a risk on me that changed the trajectory of my life."

He wrote back within the hour.

Rob,
I assure you that in my estimation there was never a risk.
That assumption you can put aside. You should be aware
that sometimes the numbers have to be put aside and one
must trust one's inner voice. In your application to Columbia you did what a lot of students with higher numbers failed
to do. You made your case and did so convincingly. All I did
was read carefully and trust you.

Of course, the locks and that wonderful business card helped as well.

Be good and keep working. And I mean this. You are why I do this job. Otherwise we could have machines crunch the admissions numbers for us.

Peter V. Johnson
Columbia Undergraduate Admissions

I have learned again and again that people *want* to help. They want to make a difference. They want to change your life. And we all *need* that help from others. We need a difference to be made. We need our lives to be changed. The key for me was figuring out how to tell my story in a way that enabled other people to see meaningful roles *for themselves* in my story.

MY ACTUAL COLLEGE APPLICATION ESSAY FOR COLUMBIA

APPLICANT: Reffkin, Robert
DATE: November 1996

Staring out of the window of the restaurant, I noticed a homeless man. I figured he was in his late sixties because he was bald, very skinny and trembled as he walked. As the man shambled past, my mother suddenly saw him, jumped up and ran outside. She rushed up to the man, he smiled, and they spoke for a short time. He, along with my mom, walked back into the restaurant and sat down. It made me proud to see my mom being so generous to this homeless stranger.

After sitting down, she looked into my eyes and said something that I will never forget. "Robert say hello to your father."

I had not seen my father for years. There had been times that I thought about him and what I would tell him if I ever saw him again, but when I saw him sitting across from me in the restaurant that day, I did not know what to say.

The next time I saw my father he was lying in a casket.

The image of this last encounter with my father is seared into my memory. My father, Eduard Rodney Lee, was a good loving man with a serious disease — drug addiction. Many of the young people that I know use drugs. They think it is cool and not dangerous. But I have seen a good man, my dad, decimated from this disease and the one that so often comes with it, AIDS. Consequently, I do not use drugs; I remain clean, sober and healthy. But the memories remain of a poor, homeless man, my father, lying in a casket. There have been times that these memories have hurt me and made it difficult for me to accomplish all that I would have liked. More often, especially as I have grown over the past few years, these memories have been a strong motivating force for me.

My father's death left me with many feelings that I did not comprehend. Simultaneously, I was thrust into an entirely new world at San Francisco University High School. This world was filled with people from affluent backgrounds, many of whom had already received educations vastly superior to mine. Intimidated by their ability to articulate ideas, I often felt stupid and backwards. I tried to overcompensate by taking the most difficult courses at UHS but my insecurities and attempts to overachieve boomeranged on me and I failed miserably. At one point, I felt like dropping out. Unable to seek help when I desperately needed it, I avoided my teachers. I never spoke to anyone at school about the pain and fear I felt as a result of my father's death.

Meanwhile, at home, my father's addiction, illness and death took an enormous financial and emotional toll on my mother. She lost her job due to health problems and I knew that I needed to help her. I wanted to do something more lucrative and inventive than the usual teenage minimum wage jobs, so I talked to a DJ at a party about his business. The idea of owning my own business really captured my imagination. With the money that I had saved over the years and the guidance of a few investors, I was able to put together enough for a small setup. I was so successful in my first year that I was quickly able to upgrade my equipment. Today, I can handle events of almost any size and have a thriving business. However, my success has brought a host of difficulties for which I was not prepared. My work life means that I often have to work late; some nights I do not get to bed until three in the morning. Since I commute three hours to school, participate on the Cross Country team, and run every day, I am often so exhausted that sometimes my alarm clock cannot even wake me up. However, I am proud that I have been able to help my mother financially, even though I have sacrificed some academic success in the process.

Being a successful DJ has also taught me that I have what it takes to succeed. I have noticed that the same sense of responsibility and self-discipline that I applied to my work life can also help me excel in my studies. I am self-confident enough that I no longer feel that I have to prove myself by taking courses to impress people rather than ones that interest me and meet my goals. My grades have begun to improve and I have disciplined myself to prepare for my SAT's, recently attaining a 1350. Additionally, my inability as a lower classman to approach a teacher for help has changed. I now view teachers as potential allies, not as authority figures to be avoided at all costs.

Over the past few years I have been involved with the Young Entrepreneurs Program at the University of California at Berkeley. The program covers many aspects of running a business including marketing, administration and creating a business plan. I was given the opportunity to present my business plan to a venture capital board and was awarded funding by them. This January, I attended the United Nations Summit 77: Young Entrepreneurs Conference on Trade, Investment and Technology Cooperation. This experience offered me a broad world view that is not available in my narrow community. Additionally, both of these experiences have taught me how to behave professionally and how to talk to people about business matters.

Two years ago, I would not have considered myself capable of being successful in a school like Columbia. Now I cannot wait to go. I find myself filled with an insatiable curiosity, desiring to read more deeply about the many subjects that are addressed in my classes. It may sound trite, but I want to go to college because I want to learn. I want to major in Economics and Political Science and eventually to get my graduate degree in International Business. I am not sure yet about the specific type of business that I would like to be involved in but I am very sure that I want it to be a business with a sense of social responsibility and one that gives back to the community. Although I am financially ambitious, money is not my overriding motivation. Instead, I seek the satisfaction of being successful and sharing this success with other people. As a young African-American I see many unsatisfied needs in our communities. I respect the people who have achieved success and who come back and make a contribution. I would like to be one of these people. I want to make a difference in my life and I feel that through running a successful business I can make that difference.

My father was a heroin addict who died of AIDS. No one from his family ever went to college. I am surrounded by people who use drugs and are following negative life paths. Perhaps my ambitions seem grandiose in someone from my background, but I am confident that I can achieve them. I have been given this confidence and inspiration by my mother and by other people who have helped me in the past. These have been my role models and it is my intention to carry on this tradition and to be a role model for other young people in the future.

It has taken me some time to deal constructively with the pain of what my father became and how he died. I regret how little we were able to talk to each other when he was alive. It is my dream to grow up and speak to my father with the success of my life. My father had given up before he died. I will not.

Why I almost failed high school physics and didn't graduate
If you can't envision success, you can't achieve it

It was the spring of 1997. I was in my final months of high school, busy with my DJ business, and already accepted into Columbia University for the fall. In my AP Physics class, the entire semester was dedicated to an independent study project that was very independent, which meant that I had chosen a topic then had done approximately . . . nothing.

As we got close to the end of the year, my teacher, Mr. Iskander, pulled me aside and told me that I was on track to fail and that if I failed his class I wouldn't graduate on time and Columbia would likely revoke my admission. So he called a meeting with me, my mom, and the head of school to discuss how to move forward.

To get a better sense of what went down, I recently reached out to Mr. Iskander to see what he remembered about that critical time in my life. This is what he shared.

I think about you often. I met you early in my career, and for me, our struggle together was the pivotal moment when I realized I had to become a teacher and not simply have the job of a teacher. So much of learning is not about compliance and following the rules, it's about believing that you can do something and not shying away from trying.

I really liked you, but I didn't really know you. That was a big part of why I didn't realize what was happening. There are lots of things at play when a student is in the classroom. They're an entire human being, who's been through a whole variety of experiences that day/week/year that are shaping them in the moment, and the student next to them might be having a completely different experience.

That a young man can go through school without being known, even by a teacher who's very fond of him, is really tragic.

In that meeting, I realized I had only been seeing one dimension of you: a reluctant physics student. From you and your mom, I learned that you were quite an accomplished businessperson at that point, running your DJ business. That had been invisible to me — and it shifted the conversation to: "You are certainly a motivated and capable person. In fact, you're probably more motivated and capable than I am. So what is getting in between you and being successful in this class?"

We established that day that you weren't expecting to do well in physics. I made you feel like you didn't belong in my class, and you didn't see the connection between what you were capable of in life and what you were able to accomplish in physics.

I had been failing you as a teacher by not helping you see that you could rise to this challenge. I was presenting an obstacle for success rather than providing an opportunity for you to thrive. You'd received lots of messages, I think, from me and other teachers, that you just weren't going to be successful in school. And I'd kept giving you the feedback that you weren't meeting expectations, confirming your own sense that it wasn't even worth trying.

So we set up a new, specific action plan that you had to follow and I committed to checking in more frequently and holding you accountable to those tasks when we met. I have to admit, I remember it as a painful adjustment for both of us. We tried to transfer your high expectations of yourself to this project — and that ultimately worked. I convinced you that you absolutely could be successful with physics, and that you just needed to believe that. You did exceptionally well. It was a really positive accomplishment.

I remember how proud I was of you graduating and having really conquered this thing. I've been to twenty-five of those graduations now, and have seen thousands of students graduate, and watching you walk across that stage and get your diploma is probably the proudest moment I've ever had at graduation. Not because I did anything, but because I watched you do something you didn't think you could do.

I was so moved to hear his memories. To this day, I have a clear image of his face in the meeting with my mom and the headmaster as he began to see me in a different light.

Mr. Iskander also recently told me how close he was to straight-up failing me in his class rather than mounting the intervention he did. "I could have done you a huge disservice in life. That feeling of responsibility—recognizing the impact of my actions—profoundly changed me as a teacher," he said.

I was taken aback. Just imagine how different my life would have been if I hadn't graduated high school—how my dream of New York and college and everything that came from that would have disappeared, slipping through my fingers right as I was about to grab on to it?

The TV ad that inspired me to apply for more than one hundred scholarships

Trying gives you a huge competitive advantage

Opportunity is all around us—but it doesn't just fall in our laps. It takes work to capture it.

When I was a senior in high school, both my mom and I were worried about how we were going to pay for my college education. Then one night I saw a late-night TV ad telling me that billions of dollars in scholarship money go unused every year and that for $19.99 I could buy a book with a complete list of all of those scholarships. It resonated with one of my core beliefs that I had even at that young age: there are more people and organizations that want to support you than you could ever possibly take advantage of.

I called up and used my own money to order that book. With my mom's help, I then spent the next several months applying for more than one hundred different scholarships.

I learned that the biggest reason that so many scholarships go unclaimed each year is because applying for them is *hard*. It takes time. You have to make the choice to sit down and write an application essay rather than doing something else that's more fun.

And when you finish one essay, you have to begin writing the next one. And the next one. And the next one.

It was also a big financial risk. The envelopes, postage, and paper alone added up to hundreds of dollars. I had to apply for all of them before hearing back from a single one. I had no idea if I'd receive *any* of the scholarships.

If you'd asked me, "Do you want to get rejected by dozens and dozens of scholarships this year?" I obviously would have said no. But I was more focused on the benefit than the cost. I kept at it because I wanted to make it to New York — then make it in New York.

While I was filling out the applications, I realized something that's proved even more important in my life than the scholarship money I did end up winning. I realized that every time I wanted to quit because something was hard or boring, someone else was having that very same feeling — and chances are, they would probably give up because of it.

Every time it felt difficult, I told myself that if I kept going my odds of landing a scholarship went up.

I ended up winning more than $50,000 in scholarships — a huge help considering that I didn't have any rich family members or anyone else to help me and my mom pay for my expensive college in an expensive city. It was just us.

Sometimes the "secret" to success is a lot of trying.

The question that helped me graduate from Columbia University in two and a half years

Don't let rules get in the way of your dreams;
most of them are bendable if you ask

Most people think that the "way things are done" is the way they *have* to be done. But if you want to move fast, it helps to understand that most obstacles that make you wait or slow you down are actually quite optional. To get around them, all you have to do is *ask*.

When I started at Columbia, I knew I wanted to finish college in under four years. Paying tuition for four years just to get to the real world seemed like an impossibly large sum of money, and I knew that there had to be a way to graduate early and spend less. But there was a school rule that said you could take no more than eighteen credit hours in any one semester, which would have kept me there for the usual eight semesters.

Rather than giving up on my dream, I went to talk to the dean and asked for an exception — giving a specific, sympathetic reason and framing it as a short-term trial to reduce the perceived risk that it would be too much for me to take on. "Since I'm paying for my education with my mom and we don't come from money," I said, "I'd like to take twenty-eight credits per semester and finish a bit sooner. Could we try that out just for this first semester then we can check in after and see how it's going?"

Because I asked for an exception, I ended up finishing Columbia in two and a half years, saving more than $50,000 in tuition, room, and board; and I embarked on the "real" journey of my life sooner than most college students.

After my first year in college, I did a Wall Street summer internship at Merrill Lynch that was designed for college juniors through the program Sponsors for Educational Opportunity. I read the program requirements but decided to apply as a first-year student anyway. I told the director of the program, Michael Whittingham, "I know I'm not a junior but I am going to graduate early from college so I don't have as many chances for an internship. I have more work experience than the average freshman. Is there any way you could make an exception here?" He didn't agree right away, but I kept making my case until I'd convinced him. I remember his telling me that I was the first freshman in the internship program.

A few years later, I became one of the youngest White House Fellows the same way. I came up with a strong case, then simply asked. I said, "Even though most White House Fellows are in their late twenties or thirties and I'm only twenty-five, because I created a business in high school and graduated from both college and business school early, I have the work experience of someone in their late twenties. If you accept me, I assure you that I will reflect well on you and the institution."

The common theme running through these examples is simple. *I made a compelling case and asked directly.*

Of course, there have been times when I've asked for an exception and haven't gotten it. Sometimes the person in charge won't bend on the rules however arbitrary they may be. But those weren't horrible experiences in the least. Here's how they went.

ME: Can I do X thing even though the rules say it's not allowed? Here's my very specific, sympathetic, and reasonable reason and here's why it's less of a big deal than you might think.

THEM: No.

ME: But here's my additional reason.

THEM: Still no. Rules are rules.

ME: Okay.

And then I went on with my life and looked for the next opportunity to make the future arrive faster — which, when you believe that obstacles are often optional, tended to come along sooner than you may think.

If I had assumed the rules were unbendable in the first place, I would have missed out on many formative experiences and been many years further behind in life than I am. To leap ahead, all I had to do was risk hearing the word "no" a few more times — a word we hear a lot in life whether we're trying to move fast or not.

How I got hired at McKinsey with a C average

Every interaction is an opportunity

As I mentioned earlier, one of the nonprofits that helped me the most in my youth was A Better Chance. It helped me gain entrance into an elite private high school and it supported me throughout my time there.

Early in my second year at Columbia, I was invited to the premiere of the movie *Beloved,* starring Oprah Winfrey. Since Oprah was also the national spokesperson for A Better Chance, they invited a group of ABC alumni. Not only was Oprah there in person, I think I saw a number of other famous people including Sean "Puffy" Combs in the room as well.

Over in the corner, looking a little awkward, was an older White guy all by himself. I had developed a habit of trying to reach out to anyone who looked out of place since I knew the feeling so well, so I went over and introduced myself. We talked for a few minutes, he shared the story of how he came to be on the board of ABC, and I took his business card. And then I forgot about it.

A year later, when I was getting ready to graduate college, I ended up being rejected for two jobs — in the same week. So I dug through my stack of business cards and found his card again.

I realized that the quiet White guy, Dolf DiBiasio, was one of the most successful senior partners at McKinsey & Company, the famed consulting firm — and I'd seen many of the students I had respected most pursue consulting jobs after graduation. So I wrote him a note, asking to meet. We set up an interview for two weeks later.

The problem: I didn't really know what consulting was. So I looked up McKinsey and read the famous *New Yorker* article, "The Kids in the Conference Room." I fell in love with the idea of working at McKinsey because it was even harder to get into than Goldman Sachs or a Wall Street bank — and the bigger the challenge, the more I want to achieve it. At that time, I had heard that McKinsey New York hired only one graduate from Columbia University to be a consultant every two years.

I'd applied for a lot of investment banking jobs in recent months and they'd all turned me down. The simple truth was that the way I was applying wasn't working and I knew it. My classes and grades were not impressive. My internships were okay — but not good enough to overcome my academic transcript.

I needed to do something new.

Something to demonstrate that I was up for the challenge and worth betting on.

Something that played to my strengths and made me stand out.

Something *memorable*.

If I didn't, I'd be throwing away a huge opportunity — and it felt like this might be my *last* opportunity.

My curiosity and desire to connect with everyone had gotten me in the door. But to actually get a job offer, I'd have to rely on a different skill: my ability to roll up my sleeves and prepare single-mindedly for a ridiculous amount of time.

So I took two full weeks off from school — without telling anyone. I just stopped going to class.

I had learned that consulting interviews were based on case studies, so I camped out at Columbia's business school library and started reading case study after case study after case study. I'd show up each day when the library opened and stay until they kicked me out. I have a vivid memory of two books in particular — the *Vault Guide to the Case Interview* and the WetFeet Insider Guide's *Ace Your Case!* — and I repeatedly read both cover to cover, and I memorized dozens of cases.

By the time I walked into my McKinsey interview, I felt like I knew the case method as well as anyone with an MBA even though I was just an undergrad.

In the room, the interviewer would ask a question — "What would you do in a situation like such and such?" — and I'd reply with an answer straight from the reading: "Well, in a case like that, I'd use the three Cs . . ."

Based on all the cases I'd studied, I aced the interview and got the job — a job that transformed my life by giving me credibility as being smart, which helped with all future opportunities I pursued.

To be clear, the lesson I took from this was not to skip weeks of school in order to memorize business school case studies. It was realizing that the more people I connected with, the more opportunities I encountered — and when an opportunity opened up in front of me, it was worth going to great lengths to capitalize on it. In a crowded and competitive world, "good enough" is generally *not* good enough. I've found that it's only by trying to do something extraordinary that you can make extraordinary things happen for yourself.

The $15,000 personal check from my manager

*At some point, you'll have a chance to
save or sink someone's future*

When I started at McKinsey, I didn't know *anything* about the world I was entering. A year earlier, I didn't know what the term "management consulting" meant. No one I'd grown up around had ever been a consultant. Unlike my more privileged classmates and colleagues, I had no idea of the "way things were done." As with most things, I'd learned more from watching movies than anything else.

Here's what I knew from experience: management consultants generally travel to a different city to be on-site with a client Monday through Thursday, then fly back home to be in the office on Friday. When you are traveling, the company puts you up at a hotel and they give you a company credit card for expenses.

Here's what I learned from movies: hot-shot business people (and, yes, I felt like a hot shot at the time) who live in hotels tend to live a good life and spend a lot of money.

Here's what I did: at the end of a long day, I'd sometimes eat at a nice restaurant then order a late-night snack from room service before going to bed. Sometimes I'd stay in the city I traveled to for the weekend rather than coming back to New York, which led to more hotel and food bills. In just a few months, I had spent $15,000 more than I was supposed to without realizing it. I don't remember anyone ever telling me there was a limit. And I didn't think I was doing anything wrong, so it never occurred to me to ask.

Here's what *could have* happened: I could have been fired for misuse of funds. You can imagine how the story would have been told. "We hired a Black kid and he tried to rip us off so we quickly canned him." Or "We hired a C student and he maxed out his company credit card so we had to fire him." I would be required to pay the money back, and since I didn't have any savings, I'd have to find someone to borrow it from. Having been fired for cause, I'd have to move back in with my mom less than a year after graduation — unemployed, deeply in debt, with no clear way to get another job.

Here's what *did* happen: my manager saw the situation, talked to me about it directly, believed what I told him, and accepted my apology. Knowing that he couldn't pass the cost off to the client, he and the partner on the team assumed the $15,000 cost *personally*. They fully erased my debt, much to my amazement. It was an incredibly generous thing for them to do for me at a pivotal moment in my life.

I believe that pivotal moments like this are much more common than most people think. I can point to at least a half-dozen times in my life in which my future hung in the balance even though I didn't realize it in the moment. If those doors hadn't been opened, if those connections hadn't been made, if those kindnesses hadn't been extended — I would not be where I am today. *No one succeeds alone.*

Now that I'm more often on the other side of the table, I'm always on the lookout for moments when I can pay forward the support I've received by giving someone else a second chance, or the benefit of the doubt, or a bit of well-timed generosity. But I've got more work to do before I will have done as much for others as I feel others have done for me.

I learned *how* to move fast before I learned *why*

Run hard to discover where you're going

I feel like I've been running my entire life. Both literally and figuratively.

As a teenager, I liked to run as a way to be alone with my thoughts and my dreams. I'd run up this dirt trail to the top of the Berkeley Hills, sit down, and stare out at San Francisco. Looking out at the big city made me feel like anything was possible.

As a high schooler, I ran because I didn't like the competition of team sports, and I wasn't very good at them anyway. But running track and cross-country made sense to me. The challenge was endless. Each day that I laced up my shoes, I went up against the only competitor I've ever really enjoyed beating: myself.

As a college student, I raced through school. Columbia is known for its extensive core curriculum that makes it challenging to finish early, but I got through it in less than three years. I wasn't doing much running those days, but I was moving as fast as I possibly could.

I had to keep going.

I had to keep moving.

And I had no idea *why*.

In New York, everyone's got a hustle. I felt it as soon as I arrived. And I loved it. The energy propelled me forward. The city that never sleeps made me feel like I never had time to rest — and I fed off that adrenaline.

I chose fast-paced industries right out of school. The drop-everything-but-work life of a McKinsey consultant. Getting an MBA in Columbia's sixteen-month accelerated program so I'd have another degree in my early twenties. Working ninety-hour weeks —

not just working weekends but spending most Saturdays working past midnight—doing investment banking at Lazard. Becoming one of the youngest White House Fellows at twenty-five.

Looking back, I was only doing what people told me was the "right thing" to do, hoping that it would make me good enough to belong. I was following big dreams. But they weren't my dreams.

I knew that running fast helped me go further, but I was directionless. I couldn't tell whether I was running toward something or away from something, so I didn't know if I was getting closer to it or further away.

I didn't realize how lost I was until I found my path—and felt the difference.

Searching for something deeper, I founded New York Needs You, a nonprofit that has helped thousands of low-income students who are the first in their families to go to college by providing career development, college support, and summer internships. (It's now gone national and changed its name to America Needs You.) It helps people who are trying to find their way, follow their path, and pursue their dreams but need help and guidance along the way.

I immediately felt more passionate and more driven than ever before because I knew the work I was doing really mattered.

The experience taught me something about myself.

Helping others realize their dreams is my dream.

Helping people make the impossible possible is my passion.

Helping people at pivotal, transformational moments in their lives is my personal mission.

The clarity of purpose I felt gave me enough energy to commit to running fifty marathons to raise money for America Needs You and the other nonprofits that had helped me.

I hadn't needed a mission to get into good schools or get hired at good companies. But because I didn't have a sense of purpose, I often felt unfulfilled and I knew I wasn't realizing my potential.

Still, moving fast had helped me learn fast even in those days when I didn't know where I was going. If nothing else, it helped me cross off wrong answers more quickly. If I'd spent ten years at McKinsey before realizing it wasn't the right job for me, it would have taken me that much longer to find my true calling.

———

EVERY

MOTHER

IS AN

ENTREPRENEUR

———

From the title of this book, you already know that I believe that no one succeeds alone. I appreciate that families form in varying ways, shapes, and sizes, but I want to honor mothers in particular because of my own personal experience.

Every mother I've ever met succeeds because she's got the same spark and spirit that I see in entrepreneurs everywhere: resourcefulness, resilience, creativity, care, passion, positivity, and an undeniable drive to help others. Mothers face insurmountable odds every day whether they're struggling to raise a child on their own or spending an entire morning simply trying to get a two-year-old to eat the food on her high-chair tray. Failure is simply not an option, and for single mothers, there's no one else to turn to for help.

For my whole life, I've been surrounded by strong mothers: my own mom, Ruth; Benís's mom, Elida; Benís herself; and now thousands of remarkable mothers in the Compass family. I've learned so much from all of these mothers and the stories they've shared with me.

From the powerful mothers who won't take no for an answer. The persistent mothers who always find a way. The supportive mothers who care for the very old and the very young while also trying to care for themselves and live their own lives. The entrepreneurial mothers who run their own businesses while also running their families and their homes.

The mothers whose children are struggling, or sick, or far away. The mothers who love men and love women and love themselves. The mothers who had to be as tough as nails but still are the first ones you'd call when you need someone to tell you it's all going to be okay. The mothers who won't spend a penny on themselves because they want to invest every last cent in the dreams and the education of their children. The mothers who are no longer with us.

The mothers who've given birth, who've adopted, who've step-mothered, who've foster-mothered, who've single-mothered, and those who've chosen not to be mothers at all and instead looked out for all the kids in the neighborhood. The mothers who do the impossible and the mothers who fight to make it all a little less impossible for the next generation.

In this section, I'll share the stories of my mother, my wife (the mother of our children), and her mother — and how their lessons taught me the principles that have defined my life ever since.

My mother's battle for independence
What would the world look like if we fanned the spark inside every child?

My mother's father was a strict authoritarian with a terrible temper and a dark view of the world, no doubt shaped by living in Jerusalem throughout the horrors of the Holocaust. He was not a happy man, and for his family, he was not an easy man to be around.

One of the few things I admire about my grandfather was his entrepreneurial spirit. He was an immigrant who built a better future for his family, bringing them to New York City from Tel Aviv in the 1950s, supporting his daughters' educations, and dedicating his life to raising a transformative amount of money to support Israel from fellow Jews across America and Europe.

My grandfather passed that entrepreneurial spirit on to my mother, Ruth, who in turn passed it on to me. But because my mother was a girl, he told her that her independence and initiative were a "cancer I have to root out in you" rather than something to celebrate.

When she became interested in building a radio in middle school using just a battery and some coils, he flew into a rage and berated her for having a passion that he thought ought to be reserved for boys.

When my grandfather found out that my mom and her long-term college boyfriend had slept together, he forced her to live at home and eat her meals alone at different times than the rest of the family. He refused to speak to her for months.

When my mother married Gene Reffkin, a young man she'd met at NYU who'd been playing club gigs as a drummer since he was fourteen, her father made them marry out of state so he didn't have to invite his friends and relatives to a ceremony that he flat-out did not support.

When Gene declined my grandfather's misguided offer to set him up with an accounting job, my grandfather was so offended and outraged that the two men almost never spoke again.

When my mother wanted to move to California, my grandfather said to her: "You're going to end up in the gutter."

None of this harsh treatment was enough to stop my mom, though. She was unstoppable. She is unstoppable. She will always be unstoppable.

Ruth charted her own path in life no matter the reaction it drew from her parents.

As early as she could, she began earning her own money by working as a secretary.

She developed her own beliefs, her own dreams, and her own principles, becoming an activist in the causes of civil rights, the antiwar movement, and feminism.

Feeling stuck in New York, Gene and my mom moved to California in the late 1960s during the same month they had attended Woodstock in order to seek freedom and a new way of life like so many others before them had done.

While she and Gene drifted apart and eventually divorced, they remained best friends. (Close enough friends that even though Gene Reffkin is not my biological father my mother kept his name after their divorce and made Reffkin my last name as well since she and my father, Lee, never married.) Even though Gene and I are not related by blood and only incidentally by sharing the same last name, he's the best godfather I could ever ask for. I feel lucky that he's still in my life to this day.

Over the years, my mother mostly dated musicians, artists, and artisans in Oakland and Berkeley, including some African American men like my father. Needless to say, and not coincidentally, this was not the future my grandfather had imagined for her.

But my mom kept on being her own entrepreneurial and independent self, imagining new possibilities then willing them into existence.

In the early 1970s, after earning a graduate degree in education, my mom started a preschool called the Unicorn School in the home she shared with a number of roommates. That school was her baby before I was born. She helped it grow and thrive, hired many of her friends to serve as teachers and assistants and directors, and when I was of preschool age, I got to attend as well. As she became known for her childcare expertise, she was hired to evaluate preschools around the state and became the early childhood director of a large Jewish community center while remaining board president of the Unicorn School, which kept going strong.

Throughout her life, my mom has always embodied hustle. She's worked interesting jobs and come up with successful side gigs. When she was pregnant with me, she worked at night as a tax preparer while still directing the Unicorn School during the day. She's started businesses, managed teams, pivoted, adapted, bounced back, and constantly kept growing. A couple of years after I was born, she went to work as an insurance agent for New York Life and excelled, first being promoted to sales manager and eventually to general manager. After being a life insurance agent, she spent two decades as a real estate agent. I'm proud to say that today she's a real estate agent at Compass, running her own small business, and having the best years of her career in her seventies.

I learned something from my mother's life story that I've relearned again and again from others: far too many people have to fight impossibly difficult battles just to get a shot at determining their own futures and living the life they want to live instead of the life that others want them to live.

My mom had no desire to be estranged from her family; deep down, no child ever does. But she wasn't willing to silence her voice or abandon her dreams in order to stay close to people who didn't want her to thrive as her full, authentic self.

It pains me that my grandfather couldn't see how similar my mom's strengths were to the best parts of him: her curiosity, her passion, her independence, her drive. All he saw were rebellion and disloyalty, and over the years, he closed off his heart to her.

She was made to feel like an outsider because she had the very same traits that Benís and I try to cultivate in our own daughters and son.

If you grew up like I did with someone on your side who believes in you and wants nothing more than to see you flourish and succeed on whatever path you chose — consider yourself extremely lucky. I know I do. But my heart breaks for what my mother went through.

What's more, the fact that my mother, my grandfather, and I share a passion for entrepreneurialism makes me wonder whether — if he had been able to see past my mother's gender and my race — we might have been able to share something special together.

How a bunch of hippies and musicians bought a house in Berkeley

You need a dream to find a home

When my mom and her then-husband Gene moved to California in the fall of 1969, their bank accounts were basically empty. That was one of the reasons they were leaving New York. For years, Gene had been working a nine-to-five job while being a working musician in New York City and the Catskills, and Ruth was working full-time and going to school at night, and they had still only managed to save up about $400. The cost of living was just too expensive.

My mom and Gene drove cross-country with all their belongings in their old beat-up Econoline van, which made it across more than ten states before breaking down in Arizona. They left the van behind and got picked up by one of the few people they knew on the West Coast, who then drove them the rest of the way to Northern California.

So how did they buy a four-apartment home in Berkeley in 1973 just a few blocks away from the famed Telegraph Avenue that they later sold for more than $1 million?

Everyone involved in buying that house, and there were a lot of them, credits one person: my mother. They did it together, but it was her idea, her dream, and she was the one who figured out how to make it possible and persuaded everyone else to join in. It was a decision none of them ever regretted.

Let me explain why her dream to buy that house was totally implausible.

First, she was trying to buy a home with three other people: her boyfriend at the time, Paul, and her not yet ex-husband and *his* new girlfriend, Arlene. And to make things even more complicated, Gene was the drummer in Paul's band. Remember: this was the Bay Area in the early '70s. Everybody got along great, but that's a pretty complex group of people to buy a home together.

Second, no one in the house had a steady job or a lot of money. Paul and Gene were musicians, and Gene also made a bit of money taking other people's trash to the dump. Arlene did some carpentry and trade work when she could get it. My mom was applying to go back to school to get a graduate degree in education. They also made small handicrafts to sell on Telegraph Avenue to tourists, but that wasn't exactly the sort of thing that would inspire confidence in a mortgage broker that you weren't likely to default on your loan.

Third, nobody but my mom even wanted to buy the place. They had all moved west in search of the feeling of liberation and freedom that was everywhere in those days, which was pretty much the opposite of signing up to make monthly mortgage payments to some bank for the next thirty years.

But my mom saw an opportunity. The four of them were already living together in a lower-middle-class Black neighborhood in Oakland, and my mom had noticed that the rents in Berkeley were rising each year while the sale prices of Berkeley homes were still pretty low. If they could buy soon, they might be able to earn themselves a bit of security and a bit of money over time if they got a place with multiple units.

My mom didn't have the resources to buy a home on her own, but she had saved up more money in the past year than she ever had before. The way she saved it is remarkable. She'd applied for a huge number of jobs the previous year and had received a letter one day offering her a job as one of the first-ever female park rangers in California. She spent a few months in Santa Cruz working at a state park, and since the hours were long and it was a long drive from Oakland, she slept in her van in the campground. That left her with almost no expenses, so she saved every penny she could.

The job wasn't a good fit for her, but when she left it after less than a year, she had enough socked away to cover most of a down payment. Their other housemate, Susan, had a bit of family money, and my mom asked her to loan some of it to the others to cover their portion of the down payment.

The others were still worried about committing to a long-term arrangement, so Ruth promised to buy out anyone's portion after the first year if they wanted to cut ties. (She actually didn't have the money to do that at the time, but she knew she'd find a way.)

So they went house hunting and found a run-down, four-unit fixer-upper on Carleton Street for $27,000 — and they bought it.

When I was born six years later, that was the house I was brought home to. Even though my mom was with my dad, Lee, by then, Gene and Paul still lived at Carleton Street and their musical gear filled the basement. The preschool on the first floor was full of life, potential, and opportunity.

All the work and all the love they'd poured into that home had transformed it into a place that defined my childhood and set the stage for my life. And it never would have happened if my mom hadn't turned her big, crazy, implausible dream into a reality.

My mother mobilized a village to raise a child
Single moms are unstoppable

My mother, like all mothers, wanted the world for her son. She wanted me to be able to grow up and go anywhere, do anything, and be whatever I wanted to be.

But she was just one person. One woman in a 1980s world. Without a partner to help shoulder the load. Without parents of her own to catch her if she stumbled. Without the safety net of wealth or resources.

She gave me a fantastic childhood. But there came a point when my mother realized that I needed more support and attention than she could provide on her own. I was energetic and impatient. Driven but a bit directionless. Hungry for experience. Ready for real life to begin.

In that situation, I can imagine a lot of parents wanting to hold on to control. When kids are babies, they need their parents for literally *everything*. As they get older, they start needing friends, then teachers, and eventually other adults who know things that they might not. It can be hard to accept that you can no longer be the one to solve all of your child's problems on your own. It can be painful to realize that your kids need guidance that you cannot provide.

And it's often even harder for single parents, who are saddled with twice the responsibility as two-parent couples and ten times as much guilt for anything they think they're not doing right.

There was also the fact of my skin color. Energetic, impatient White boys are often seen as ambitious future leaders. Energetic, impatient Black boys are often seen as disruptive and dangerous. I'd started getting in trouble in school and spending more time with friends who she thought were going to be a bad influence, most of whom never ended up graduating from high school.

My mom knew that she had to help me channel my energy in a way the world would understand and that would allow me to be successful.

I was lucky that she had a fierce entrepreneurial spirit like so many single moms. She'd lived enough to know that problems would inevitably arise, and she knew herself well enough to know that she wouldn't rest until she'd solved them.

So she picked up the phone and started calling everyone she could think of to ask about programs and resources to help guide me through my teenage years. Since she didn't have well-connected family members or rich friends to turn to, she set out to find every nonprofit, scholarship, mentor, and advisor she could possibly find to help me expand my ambitions and make plans to achieve them.

She found Summer Search, a nonprofit that connected me to summer enrichment programs, like the National Outdoor Leadership School and Global Horizons USA, through which I participated in a humanitarian volunteer project in Guadeloupe. Later,

Summer Search helped me get my first internship at Dodge & Cox, a financial institution where one of the Summer Search board members worked.

She discovered the National Foundation for Teaching Entrepreneurship, which was running a summer program for teens at the Haas School of Business, where I won the business-plan contest. The newspaper photograph of me in full dreadlocks holding the certificate they gave me is one of my most prized possessions.

There was A Better Chance, which, as you know, I'd heard about first from my barber. The organization helped me apply to private high schools, provided mentorship during those years, and hosted an event during college where I met the person who hired me after graduation.

Without these organizations, and a handful of others that also helped me, there's simply no chance I'd be where I am today. They encouraged me to dream big when others told me to give up. They were the ones who helped me get my first suit for my first interview with a finance firm, which had been donated by one of their volunteer mentors.

I don't think of entrepreneurs as simply people who start businesses. To me, everyone who works hard to create a better future, takes big risks in hopes of big rewards, perseveres in the face of adversity, solves problems no matter how intractable they seem, and helps others achieve their dreams is an entrepreneur.

My mother has been an entrepreneur every single day of her life.

It was her entrepreneurial spirit that helped me build the network and gain the support I needed. It was her entrepreneurial spirit that showed me what it meant to be an entrepreneur. It is her entrepreneurial spirit that I try to emulate every day of my life.

Moms often have no choice but to make the impossible possible

When there's no one else, mothers find a way

The challenges I faced in my own childhood and the hurdles my mother faced in her childhood pale in comparison to the struggles my mother-in-law, Elida, faced. In fact, neither Elida nor her own mother got to have a childhood at all.

Elida's mom was just thirteen years old when Elida was born in the Dominican Republic. Her husband died in a car accident when Elida was nine, which pushed Elida's mother into a deep depression. When Elida's mom was lucid, she would terrorize and physically abuse Elida, frequently in public, often with a chain. When her mother was out of commission, Elida, still a young child herself, was left to raise her three younger siblings on her own.

When she was eighteen, Elida shared with her mom that she had become intimate with her boyfriend. That same night, her mom packed her things, dropped her off at his house, and told him that she now belonged to him. Within a year, Benís was born.

After months of struggling, Elida had a moment of clarity while holding baby Benís: she saw an endless cycle unfolding in front of her eyes — and she wanted so much more for Benís. A better life. Opportunity. Education. Freedom. Choice. All of a sudden, it was just the two of them in her eyes. Nothing else mattered.

But what was she going to do? Her education had ended before high school. She had no savings or resources. She had hastily married her husband, who was a decade older than she was, and while he was a decent man, he was certainly not ready to settle down and be a good husband or father at that point.

So, during one of the times when he was out of town for days on end without any explanation, Elida started to hatch a plan. And before anyone realized what was happening, she'd put her plan into action.

Fast forward one year, and Elida had left her husband and found a way to move herself, Benís, and her new boyfriend from the Dominican Republic to Yonkers, New York, where Benís grew up. (Elida had lived in Puerto Rico for many of her teen years, and Benís had been born there, which made that huge life change a little bit easier to arrange.)

In America, Elida raised Benís with hardly any money, without being able to speak English, and without any real community or family to rely on. They had a rocky road to walk together throughout Benís's childhood; a history of stolen childhoods and abuse doesn't disappear overnight.

Following the biggest dream of every parent — to give her children a chance at a life that's a little better than hers — Elida succeeded beyond her wildest imaginations. The life Benís has lived, and that our children are living, is unrecognizable in comparison to the one Elida and her mother experienced. Even though she had basically nothing to help her along the way, Elida successfully broke the cycle.

Elida had known that America was the land of opportunity without even knowing what those opportunities were. She believed that education was the key to getting ahead, and she always supported Benís's education even though she hadn't had the chance to pursue her own.

Every parent knows that feeling of gazing down at a baby who's looking up at them and realizing that they've got to be more responsible and resourceful than they've ever been before. They've got to be the grown-up — even if that means they have to do a whole lot of growing up very quickly.

As a parent, the buck stops with you. A human life is in your hands. There's no instruction manual. Everything that seemed impossible yesterday suddenly becomes necessary today.

It's similar to a feeling you experience running your first business. There comes a day, usually pretty early on, when you realize that even though each day feels like a team effort and that success and progress would not be possible without every member of the team collaborating together, the big stuff all comes back to you at the end of the day. Everyone else is putting their passion and energy into the project, but there's a category of life-or-death things that only you have to worry about. Payroll. Legal. Existential risks.

In those moments, I think about my own mother and all the mothers I've been lucky enough to get to know in my life. They've taught me that when I need to solve a seemingly intractable problem or get out of a seemingly impossible situation the answer is simple: I accept that I am the grown-up now, and no matter how difficult the challenge is, I have to just go ahead and get it done.

Benís's heartbreaking first playdate on the other side of town

It doesn't solve everything, but education is key to every solution

My mother-in-law hadn't received much education or familial support in life, but Elida didn't let that or anything else stop her from doing everything she could to give Benís a good life.

Their life in Yonkers was not easy. They lived in Section 8 housing in a rough neighborhood with a stepfather who didn't step up and eventually moved out, along with his two children from a previous marriage. They wore donated clothes and bought groceries with food stamps. Benís went to the nearest public school, which, like schools in poor neighborhoods across the country, was underfunded and underperforming.

But Benís was so smart that you could spot her spark from across the room — no matter how overcrowded it was. One of her elementary school teachers took Elida aside one day and urged her to transfer Benís to a better school in a more affluent part of town. The city was trying to integrate its schools through bussing, and in the second grade, Benís found herself taking a one-hour bus ride to and from a school in a predominantly White neighborhood each day.

At the new school, she was one of three kids of color in her class. She began to make friends with well-off White kids — but for years, her mom wouldn't let her get too close to any of them or have playdates. Having survived some traumatic experiences as a young girl, Elida was very protective as a mother. When Benís was invited to birthday parties, Elida would come, too, and stay the whole time.

In addition, she never let Benís's White friends come over to her house to avoid the humiliation of having their parents either say no out of fear or yes out of guilt.

In third grade, when Benís was eight years old, after a months-long campaign of begging and pleading, her mother allowed her to have her first one-on-one playdate with a friend who lived near her school (though Elida stayed at the playdate for the whole time). It was in December, just before Christmas, and the girl's family had a stunning tree that looked like it belonged in the window of Macy's or Saks. As a child, Benís would travel into Manhattan to see trees like that in stores and this family had one right in their living room. Benís's friend's bedroom was like something you'd see in a TV show, filled with matching furniture and stocked with pretty dolls.

Aside from the gorgeous stuff, Benís noticed that the family had an attitude that they could *have* whatever they wanted and *be* whoever they wanted to be. There was light streaming in the huge windows in every room, but there was also a lightness with which her friend and her family carried themselves.

It was Benís's first real exposure to the relative affluence of the middle class — and the comfort that comes with it.

After the playdate, Benís and Elida walked past the family's fancy new car to get into their beat-up ten-year-old Chevy. They rode home in silence. Inside their house, Benís started crying. "Why can't we have a nicer car? Why can't our house look like that? Why can't we have all those things? Why can't *we* be more like *them*?"

Her mom started to cry, too. "I'm sorry. *I'm so sorry.* I want to give you those things but I just can't." She talked about how she'd never gotten an education and how she had had children too young. How if she'd had more schooling and been able to do things differently, she could have provided more.

It was then that Elida said the words that defined the rest of Benís's life: "But if you work really hard and you do really well in school, you can have these things. If you get an education, you can have anything you want." Over time, Benís learned that it was a little more complicated than that — that education wasn't always fair and that she'd have to be much smarter and work much harder to receive the same advantages in life as others. But her mother's words set her on the right path.

Benís was already a good student as a third grader. But in the years that followed, when fitting in socially feels like the most important thing and being studious can get you teased, Benís turned being a dedicated student into her entire identity. She tested into a gifted and talented school in sixth grade and thrived there.

Starting in ninth grade, Benís had no option except the underfunded neighborhood high school. Most girls dressed in Juicy Couture velour tracksuits, but Benís arrived in business casual, wearing khakis and collared shirts as a fourteen-year-old. She listened actively and took notes in every class, so her teachers praised her publicly and everyone else called her a teacher's pet. By her own admission, she wasn't "cool" — but she learned not to mind. Even though only 25 percent of the students graduated from that school, and most graduates didn't even consider college, she was focused on getting good grades so she could get into the best college possible.

Benís earned her place as one of the top students in her class while also working nights and weekends at the local country club to help ends meet at home. When she was admitted into NYU, the people she served as a waitress were amazed because all that many of them could see in her was another service worker with brown skin. But no one who'd gone to school with her was surprised at all.

How my wife lost herself and then found herself again
The first year of our second daughter's life and the importance of home

When we decided to have a second child, Benís told me that she thought we needed a larger apartment with another bedroom. But I was worried about increasing our monthly costs. It was still early days at Compass, and the company's future was very uncertain. Roughly 90 percent of all start-ups fail after all.

Plus, we'd both been living in tiny studio apartments when we'd met. Now we had a thousand-square-foot two-bedroom place that still felt big enough to me when I came home each night, exhausted, kicked off my shoes, and fell asleep.

I convinced Benís that we should wait until she actually got pregnant before making a move. Then, once she was pregnant, I said aloud what I'd been feeling all along: "We just can't. We can't afford to move right now. Let's try to make it work here." She mourned her vision of how she wanted to expand our family for a week straight, but I didn't see any other way financially.

What I didn't realize at the time was how lost Benís felt at that point in her life.

Through an unfortunate series of events, she had lost her job while pregnant with our first child, Raia, and hadn't had the time or energy to get back into the workforce. Not working outside the home for the first time in her life was a huge blow to her sense of purpose. Benís is a woman with big dreams and the hustle and brains to make them come true no matter the obstacles. Every teacher had seen her spark. Every employer had been impressed by her initiative. Suddenly, her daily commute was only from one room to the other in our small New York apartment and her only colleague during the day still wore diapers. And I wasn't there to help very much since I was working very long days trying to get Compass off the ground.

Benís had always wanted to be a mother — but she hadn't expected the rest of her identity to vanish the moment she gave birth.

And then she had our second daughter in January of 2016. We brought Ruby home to a New York apartment that suddenly felt much smaller. At nine days old, Ruby got sick with the common but highly contagious respiratory virus RSV and had to be readmitted to the hospital for several days. But not before Benís and Raia caught it as well.

By the end of the first month of having two young kids, things were very far off the rails.

Months of sleeplessness drove Benís to a breaking point. She'd wanted a larger place so we could have enough bedrooms to sleep train the baby as soon as possible, and without that, Benís ended up so physically exhausted that she could hardly think straight. She felt trapped. Even after both girls were sleeping through most of the night, she'd wake up sensing that the girls needed her only to find them fast asleep — until she'd fallen back to sleep, that is, at which point they'd wake up and cry for her. She wasn't getting more than an hour or so of sleep at a time. It's hard to say for sure whether it was a full-on depression or just the cumulative effects of long-term sleep deprivation, but a darkness set in for Benís that was hard to shake.

As for me, I was scared. I didn't know what to do or how to help. So when she had what seemed to be a full breakdown, and with tears falling down her face, she said to me, "Rob, I need to hire someone to help," it was actually a huge relief. It was a path. A solution — or at least part of one.

We'd never paid anyone to help with the kids at all. But after several difficult weeks, she wanted to try out a night nurse. Benís asked the first woman who picked up the phone: "Can you come tonight?" And she did.

Within a week of getting the rest she so desperately needed, Benís started feeling like a person again. With enough sleep, Benís was able to start making plans and solving problems. She also hired a therapist who helped her think beyond the present moment and start envisioning her future again.

The therapist asked, "What would improve your situation

most?" and Benís returned to the idea of getting more space and another bedroom. It had been more than a year since she told me what she needed, and no matter how hard she had tried to make do, her needs hadn't changed. I told her that if she could make the math work on our expenses by cutting back in other areas we could do it. And just like that, her spark reignited and she launched back into her "get it done" mode. Two months later, we were living in a three-bedroom apartment.

I was consumed with work at that time, so it took me a few weeks to notice how much things changed once we'd settled into the new home. But one day I came home, and said, "Why are you so happy?"

She said: "Look around." It was night and day, our life in the new apartment. Ruby and Raia each had their own rooms, and they were both sleeping through the night. (Benís had sleep trained Ruby in record time once she'd had the space to do so.) All four of us were well rested. Benís had a babysitter coming in a few hours each day and was starting to lay the groundwork for the next chapter in her career: combining her psychology degree, her work experience in executive search, her MBA in leadership and strategy, and her new appreciation for therapy to launch her own life coaching and executive coaching business.

Everything had changed when we'd found the right home. More physical space had opened up more mental and emotional space for Benís. That one change had improved our quality of life immeasurably.

She'd been right all along.

The irony, of course, was that I spent my long days talking to real estate agents and software engineers about the impact that finding the right home can have on your life. But I was not the type to notice my own surroundings or appreciate the comforts of my own home. I dream of the future more than I notice the present.

I'd been blind to something that everyone in my life was trying to share with me.

Benís is a phenomenal and loving mother and our kids are so lucky to get to learn from her every day. She's also an insightful coach and professional guide, as I've been lucky enough to experience at every step in my own journey. And when she's able to do both at once — in a home that allows her to thrive both domestically and professionally — she's unstoppable.

I've learned so much from her over the years, and I'm happy that this is one lesson she's taught me that I'm now able to share with so many others through Compass.

I know the right home can change your life because it changed ours.

The most important thing my wife ever said to me
Accepting people's flaws frees them up to be their best selves

Guilt is not a helpful feeling. It makes you feel bad without leading to action or change. Yet, in almost every relationship I have ever had, I've always felt extremely guilty about how much time I spent working and how much of my nonwork time I spent daydreaming about the future instead of being in the present with the woman I was dating.

One ex-girlfriend told me to slow down and not work so hard, but I didn't really know how since I was so passionate about my work. When I tried it, it didn't feel good or make me happy. Another one wanted to go out partying much more than I had time to because I wanted to focus on creating my future and making progress toward all of the possibilities I dreamed of. Every girlfriend told me to be in the here and now, but my brain didn't seem to be able to do that. My thoughts always raced forward, and I was never content to sit still in one place for too long.

I spent so many years feeling bad that I wasn't able to be the way everyone I dated seemed to want me to be. But I just couldn't.

Then I met Benís. At first, she also struggled with how much I worked and how often my mind wandered to my dreams of the future, and she thought I had lost interest in her. Rather than play mind games, though, she asked me directly: "Are you into me anymore?" I was so glad and grateful that she did because it was the first time we seriously talked about the way I am wired, how my mind works, and how much I really *was* into her.

As my love for her grew, I found myself dreaming big for her, too — dreaming up ideas of what she could be or create. We grew together, but when I pushed too hard and seemed to want a dream more than she did, she would push back, and say: "You have to take me as I am." Benís had learned from previous relationships that you cannot change someone into the person you want them to be. She had been accepting me all along and she wanted the same in return.

I knew then that I had found a true partner: intelligent, compassionate, and strong. Someone to build a life with. Someone I wanted to be the mother of my children.

Several years after I married Benís and we had children, someone asked me during a Shabbat dinner, "If you could, what would you change about yourself?" I had no trouble answering because not being more present and in the moment was the thing I hated most about myself, and I have always thought I would be happier if I could do that.

Benís jumped in, and said, "I don't think it's true that you would be happier. It's just who you are. When your mind is in the zone and you're working with others to make dreams come true, *that's* when I have seen you the happiest. You are so 'in the moment' then. Why try and change that?"

This was an epiphany. I needed to stop the self-critique and accept myself for who I was. If my wife could accept me, why couldn't I? This allowed me for the first time to not feel bad about being myself: someone who works hard, rarely lives in the present, and always dreams about the future.

Now, rather than making me feel guilty for all the time we're not together, Benís works with me to make sure the time we *do* get to spend together is really wonderful. Rather than counting the minutes, we've learned to make the minutes *count*. I cherish the time I get to spend with her and our three children. I know those are the moments I'm going to remember when I'm looking back on my life in my rocking chair in, I imagine, San Diego. And I also know that because of who I am I'll also need to spend a lot of time between now and then working and striving to make that future possible.

Benís knows my traits are not, of course, all good traits — I can be restless, relentless, driven, impatient, opinionated, distracted — but they are all *me*.

She accepts me the way I am in part because it fits well into the way she is.

Benís is an unusually strong and self-possessed person. She knows herself. She stands up for herself, she fights for what she cares about, and she lets slide those things she doesn't. She's as happy to do projects on her own as she is to do them with others. She supports me and guides me — and also spends a lot of time doing her *own* thing and running her own business as a coach.

She models a powerful form of acceptance in our marriage and with our children. She's taught me and our children so much about how to be people — and we all continue to learn from her every day.

Of course, there's no right way to be or right way to be with another person. There are no universal answers to these questions. There are only the ways that are right for you and the people around you. But I'm glad that when I found someone who accepted me fully, and whom I could accept fully in return, I never let go.

What my kids taught me about my mom
None of us got where we are on our own

We're all working so hard, always moving forward, doing whatever's most urgent. But even as we dream big and move fast and obsess and learn, we can't let the urgent get in the way of the *important.*

What's important is family.

What's important are relationships.

What's important is love.

Benís and I never knew that we could love anything as much as we love our children. The feeling of loving someone completely, deep in your bones, before you even get to know them — is like nothing else in the world. We love them just for existing. Just for being themselves. And we always will.

On some level, that's all any of us ever want or need.

I remember being on the maternity floor for all three births, seeing all the other partners look at their wives with the same awe and adoration I was feeling for Benís. Seeing grandparents meeting their first grandchild for the first time. Hearing older siblings ask how to hold their new little brother or sister.

Bringing a new child into the world is the most ordinary and the most extraordinary thing that we do as humans. It focuses our attention on how beautiful life is and how beautiful love is. It brings us back to what matters: human connection.

Becoming a parent helped me understand my mom in a whole new way.

Seeing all the work that Benís and I (and our mothers) put into our children's lives makes me even more grateful for everything that my mom did to raise me as a single mother.

None of us became who we are on our own.

None of us got to where we are on our own.

We owe so much gratitude to the people who've supported us, cared for us, listened to us, believed in us, inspired us, and picked us up when we've fallen. We've counted on them and relied on them. And when it really mattered, they were there for us.

That's what family means to me. The people in your corner. The people who've got your back. The people who love you no matter what.

Whether that's the family you grew up with, your family today, the family you're going to build for tomorrow — or whether it's your friends who are even closer than family — they are the people who've helped make you who you are and made it possible for you to be your best self.

It doesn't always work out so easily. Family is also drama and loss. I didn't know my father — he was abusive to himself and others. My grandparents disowned us.

For every parent who works so hard to help their kid find the right path, there is another parent who demonstrates through their actions what the *wrong* path looks like — inspiring their child to sprint in the opposite direction.

Either way, they shape us.

In our society, it's easy to forget how interconnected we all are. It's easy to think it's all about you — how hard you work and how smart you are. But we're all running one single leg in a relay race that began long ago and will continue long after we're gone. And if you look to your left and your right, you'll see people all around you running together toward a common goal.

It's important to acknowledge how much we owe to others for a number of different reasons.

- Because it's undeniably true
- Because it takes some weight off our shoulders to realize that we don't have to do everything on our own
- Because it allows us to see everyone else and the role they are playing in our lives and that we are playing in their lives

When you understand that no one succeeds alone, you appreciate everyone who played a part in your story.

I'm deeply grateful. To Benís. To my children, Ruby, Raia, and River. To my mom. To my mother-in-law, Elida. To my teachers and mentors and advisors. To everyone at Compass who gives people a sense of place and belonging in homes and neighborhoods across the country. And to everyone who's reading this book right now and dreaming of a better life for themselves and their families.

NO ONE
SUCCEEDS
ALONE

So many people have asked me how I've "done it" and the answer is *I didn't do it alone.*

I've had more mentors than anyone else I know. Perhaps because I didn't have a father, I sought out more meaningful relationships with mentors than others did and stayed close to the ones who really seemed to care about me.

My mom was my first mentor — and the most significant.

But I wouldn't have made it through elementary school without the encouragement of people like my fifth grade teacher who looked past my skin color and saw my potential.

I wouldn't have gotten into (or out of) one of the best private high schools in San Francisco without the support of a half-dozen nonprofits that taught me about college, entrepreneurship, and how to obsess about every possible opportunity.

I wouldn't have gotten into (or out of) Columbia and built a professional network without minority internship nonprofits like Sponsors for Educational Opportunity and the mentors who challenged me not just to dream but to dream bigger.

I wouldn't have figured out the worlds of consulting, investment banking, politics, or finance without the help of literally dozens of mentors who helped me get in the door, figure out how each firm worked, then find my way to the next opportunity when it was time (and before it was too late).

I wouldn't have made the leap to starting my own technology company without the mentorship of our first investor, Adebayo "Bayo" Ogunlesi; the partnership of my cofounder, Ori Allon; and the wise counsel and unending emotional support I received from Benís.

And without the ingenuity, experience, and guidance of our agents and employees, Compass would never have become what it is today: one of the largest real estate technology companies in the country—a company that empowers real estate agents to achieve their entrepreneurial potential, simplifies the process of buying and selling a home, and helps everyone find their place in the world.

They are all my mentors now.

I've learned so much from my mentors about life, business, family, success, and happiness. In this section, I'll share some of what I've learned about mentorship itself—and introduce a few of the mentors who've had the largest and most lasting influence on my life.

My toughest mentor sent me to live in the woods at age seventeen
Find someone to give you the critical feedback others won't

There I was, hundreds of miles from home, in the middle of a dense forest, at an elevation of more than six thousand feet, with eleven other teenagers and one guide who couldn't have been older than twenty-five. I had one of those corny outdoorsman hats with a neck strap and a full brim pulled down over hair that would soon be a full-blown Afro. I'd swapped my sneakers for some rented hiking boots and my trademark boom box for a forty-pound backpack filled with clothes, a first-aid kit, and some nearly inedible powdered food. It was already midafternoon and we had another five miles to hike before making camp and cooking our own dinner over a fire we'd have to light with just a single match.

The craziest part: I'd *chosen* to be there. In fact, I'd had to work my butt off to convince a woman with impossible-to-meet standards to help me get a full scholarship to go on this National Outdoor Leadership School trip in the first place.

The thing about a NOLS trip is that there's no turning back once it begins. As in life, the only way out is moving forward one step at a time, working hard together, and never giving up. No excuses. No shortcuts. No exceptions. You can practically feel your character being built with every step you take wearing that heavy backpack.

Linda Mornell, the founder of the nonprofit Summer Search that got me into that NOLS trip that summer, had a mission in life: to find people who'd faced some disadvantages and enable them to have the transformational summer experiences that more privileged kids got all the time.

Along the way, she gave out a lot of free advice that turned out to be immensely valuable.

I remember once, back in the days when people used landline telephones and answering machines, I had left Linda a short voice mail. The next time she saw me, she said: "Don't EVER leave a message without leaving your name, number, and a time frame to call you back because then you're making it my problem. And make sure you're sitting by the phone at that time you told me to call."

She was strict like that. But she was also right. Even today, the heart of her advice holds: be respectful of other people's time and make sure that you always do what you say you'll do.

Linda also coached me on how to tell my own life story with more vulnerability and emotion so the kinds of people who could help me would easily see me as someone worth investing their time in. She'd ask questions such as "What does it feel like that your dad isn't around?" When I'd say something superficial like "I miss him," she'd say, "But did you ever really know him? How does it make you feel that you never got that chance?"

Some of my friends didn't like being pushed like that, but rather than looking for a reason to write her off, I looked for the wisdom in what she was saying and trying to do. I learned that figuring out how to let other people see the side of you that they want to is a great way to connect with mentors—but, more important, it's also the heart of sales. And business. And almost all professional communication.

Maybe the greatest lesson Linda taught me was that if I waited for the perfect person to give me constructive criticism in a way that's easy for me to hear I'd be waiting a long time and I'd miss out on a lot of learning. But if I could learn to brush off their tone and their delivery and look for the valuable advice underneath it, I would learn more and I'd get better much more quickly.

The reality is that honest feedback is a gift, but most people hate it, so people usually avoid giving it—especially to people who are disadvantaged in life. The probability of getting constructive feedback from any given person is really low. I feel lucky that I got to meet Linda Mornell early enough in my life to benefit from her wisdom for decades afterward.

The things Benís couldn't know as the child of a first-generation immigrant
The real rules of the game are never written down

Throughout her youth, Benís had to work twice as hard to succeed because she didn't know what she didn't know. Imagine how hard it would be to learn the unwritten rules of a society when your parent can't even read the ones that are written down.

The very first time Benís saw the SAT was when she sat down to take the test — unlike all the kids who knew to buy SAT preparation books and attend SAT prep classes. In college, she didn't realize that her well-off classmates were doing summer internships and making connections that would likely have a much bigger impact on their professional lives than any class she took or high grade she received. She didn't have time to socialize or do extracurriculars because by age fifteen she was working at a country club, a job she kept until she graduated from NYU seven years later.

Across the country in Berkeley, California, I had a mother who had immigrated to America from Israel as a child and therefore had been lucky enough to learn English at a young age, get a college education, and develop a clear understanding of how the game was played.

As a single mother without a family to lean on, my mom had to declare bankruptcy at one point in my youth. But she knew how the system worked. My mom was aware — painfully aware, in some cases — of all the things my classmates had access to that we didn't. And when she advocated for me to people in authority, the fact that she was White helped her be taken seriously and listened to rather than written off.

In short, I had it better than Benís. But I still didn't have a quarter as much privilege or access to opportunity as the wealthy White kids I knew. They had what I like to call a "rich-kid's network" — a way to get ahead thanks to connections and highly placed friends who could do favors for them. A group of people ready to provide wisdom, advice, access to jobs, internships, opportunities, letters of recommendation, scholarships, and more.

Since I didn't have any of that, I created my own network. And it helped me immensely. And you can, too.

My network started with the nonprofits that my mom connected me to in order to help enrich my life and broaden my horizons in late middle school and high school. The people who ran those organizations became part of my network, and the doors they opened for me gave me access to many more connections. And it grew from there. Even as a teenager who wasn't sure if I was going to college or not, I always put real effort into building relationships — and I've never regretted it for an instant.

HOW TO CREATE YOUR OWN RICH-KID'S NETWORK

There are two parts of a rich-kid's network: being the sort of person people want to help, and finding people with access who want to help you.

PART 1: Be the sort of person people want to help

For rich kids, this is easy. People want to help rich kids in part because they are trying to make a good impression on their parents, who are, by definition, rich. After all, if you're looking for a favor from someone, the best way to get it is to do something nice for their kids. So they'll give a rich kid an internship because they hope their parents will give ***their*** kid an internship.

For the rest of us, it's a little different. To be the sort of person people want to help, you have to show them that:

1. You're a good person (which means that you need to show your humanity and tell your story in a way that helps them see you and care about you even if you're from a different background)
2. If they help you, you'll make them look good (rather than bad)
3. Your dream is worth supporting (it can't just be "I want to make a lot of money so I have a lot of money")
4. You'll provide a good return on their investment of time (you'll be respectful of their time, you'll use the advice they share, you'll help them see and feel the impact they had on you)

PART 2: Find people with access who want to help you

Start by thinking about the people you know who might be in a position to help you. Then think about the people they might know who could be even more helpful.

Some people to consider: Your friends' parents. People in your religious or community organization. Board members of a nonprofit in your area. Your teachers. Leaders and executives where you work.

Maybe none of the people you're able to connect to directly can provide you with the specific access and opportunities you need. But if you ask them for life and career advice and treat them well in that interaction — and especially if you can find a way for them to look good to others in the process — they'll remember it and be more inclined to introduce you to everyone they know.

Then your rich-kid's network will grow exponentially. If you reach out to three people, and they each connect you to two people, that's six. Repeat that again and you're at twelve. Then twenty-four Then forty-eight. And soon you'll barely have time to keep up with the correspondence, much less the doors they're opening for you.

How the family Benís babysat for made it possible for her to go to college
If you help people, they'll want to help you

When the country club where Benís worked as a teenager announced that it was going to close for many months for major renovations, she knew she needed a new source of income. As a sixteen-year-old, Benís relied on that money both to help out her mom and give herself the tiny amount of independence she had at that age.

So when a member of the country club asked if she wanted to babysit, she jumped at the opportunity. The family's home was breathtaking, a mansion that looked like an Italian villa that was also designated as a historical landmark. Benís ended up babysitting for their three children for the next few years even after the country club reopened and she returned to work as a waitress.

During that time, she kept doing exceptionally well in school, and two years later, she was accepted to NYU. But she didn't receive nearly enough financial aid to be able to pay for it. Her mother's income from her US Postal Service job was a few thousand dollars more than the limit to qualify for a full scholarship.

Benís and Elida took a day trip into New York City to meet with the financial aid officer in person. But no matter how they made their case, the cost of tuition, books, and fees every semester was going to be tens of thousands of dollars more than they could pay — even with Benís continuing to live at home and commuting from Yonkers each day as she did all four years of college rather than getting the "real" college experience of living in the dorms.

Worse, because of the family's nonexistent assets and poor credit, Benís couldn't even take out the loans to cover the huge financial gap unless, the financial aid officer mentioned, she could find someone else to take responsibility for seeing that the loans were paid in full in case Benís defaulted.

Benís and her mom walked out the door, sat down on a bench in Washington Square Park, and cried together. Elida, who had gotten her GED late in life and taken a few courses at a community college, suggested that Benís accept reality and start with community college as well then try to transfer to NYU to at least get her degree from there, if not her education. Getting a bachelor's degree would still be a major step up from what her mother had achieved.

But Benís had set her sights higher and wasn't going to give up just yet. She decided she had to find someone to cosign for her loans. It was a huge ask and a huge risk for anyone to take.

The next week, when she was babysitting, she set the kids up with an activity and came into the living room to talk to the father, Marty. Palms sweating, Benís explained the situation and asked if he'd be willing to help her. As he paused before answering, Benís ran through their entire relationship in her mind. He'd helped her out by hiring her, but for the last few years, she'd been the one helping him, caring for his children, helping them learn and grow, and talking them through social and interpersonal problems they were having. They all loved Benís. Would he see that? Or would he balk at being on the hook for such a large amount of debt?

Marty decided to cosign her loans. As he saw it, she'd earned his trust — and his gratitude. He was willing to take on the financial risk so she could pursue a great education and keep chasing her dreams.

My favorite part of this story, though, is the next part. Because I like to believe that generosity is contagious.

Years later, after Benís had graduated from NYU (with a staggering $130,000 in student debt) and the children had grown up and graduated from college themselves, she was able to return the favor, helping make recommendations and connections and finding jobs and internships for all three children. Their youngest, Daisy, is currently one of the top strategic growth managers at Compass.

Benís and the family learned a valuable lesson from this experience. The people you help may one day be in a position to help *you*. When you choose to be generous, your generosity is sometimes repaid in more ways you can anticipate.

The family that helped Benís didn't expect to get paid back. They probably believed it would end up *costing* them money. But in the end, everyone ended up ahead.

How to build relationships with one hundred mentors
When you're hungry for guidance, it's relatively easy to find

I've had more mentors than anyone I know. Without a father in my life, I grew up hungry for advice — which gave me a reason to make my relationships with mentors more personal and more meaningful than the average mentor-mentee relationship.

Over time, I developed three simple principles about mentorship that might be helpful as you look for mentors on your journey — or even as you guide young mentees.

1. **Giving, not just getting.** I learned to always provide the mentor with at least one bit of information that she/he wouldn't have had otherwise.

Mentors tend to be older than you and work with other older-than-you people. Coming in with a perspective from your generation that you know they'll be able to share with their colleagues is a great way to immediately provide value.

Now that I'm sometimes in a mentor role, here's how one of my mentees at Compass recently gave me a valuable insight. She said, "A lot of people in the company are feeling like we should have more regular all-company meetings." That was very useful for me to hear, and I was able to act on it immediately.

2. **Taking their advice so they know their time was used wisely.** When I was a mentee, I always made sure to get at least one piece of advice that I could put into action within a month.

I'd ask, "Do you think I should interview at X place?" If my mentor said yes, I'd follow their advice then circle back and tell them how it went. This made it clear that I valued their wisdom and made them feel invested in my success.

Remember, these people are unbelievably busy. And yet people waste their time *all the time.* I wanted to make sure that in *my* interactions with them, they felt like I was respecting their time.

3. **Asking for personal life advice — not just professional career advice.** Though at first I was nervous to do so, I saw my mentorship relationships change when I began asking personal questions.

I'd ask questions like "How do you know when you have found

the person you should marry?" Or "How do you balance work and family?"

At first, I would only ask the life-advice questions right at the end—even though it was what I craved the most at that time. It turned out, though, that my mentors actually wanted to give personal advice more than professional advice. People are people regardless of how successful they are, and most people have more fun talking about topics that don't feel like work.

After each interaction, I'd send both an email and a hand-written thank-you note within twenty-four hours, and mention the specific bit of advice that had seemed most valuable. (If I was worried my letter wouldn't get there within a day, I'd often FedEx it to make sure the memory of our conversation was still fresh.)

A month later, I'd email them to tell them how I'd actually used their advice and I'd share how it had helped me.

Then, a month or so after that, I'd send an email saying something like "The advice you provided when we last met helped me in X way. I always get so much out of our conversations together. Would you be open to meeting again this month or next?"

They all wrote back and met for a second time. And a third and a fourth.

Those mentors helped me so much throughout my career. With advice, with connections, with support, and with friendship.

I promise you that this mentor strategy will work just as well for you as it did for me.

Now I know this all sounds a little strategic. But it's not a trick or a game—it works because it's the result of *actually thinking about what mentors get out of the exchange* and making sure to deliver that to them.

I didn't come up with my approach to mentorship out of thin

air. I honed it over many years by carefully observing what helped me connect more deeply with individual people. Anything that worked once, I tried again. If it worked a second time, I started doing it every time.

I also did some of my learning the hard way by getting direct feedback from mentors on how to become better.

Like when I emailed a thank-you note to the legendary Vernon Jordan, who was a partner at Lazard at the time. Within minutes, my phone rang. It was his assistant, Jeannie Adashek. "Let me give you some advice," she said. "Don't just send an email to Mr. Jordan. When you meet with someone like him, you should take out a pen and paper and send a real note." The next time I saw her, she took me downstairs to the Crane & Co. store at the bottom of Rockefeller Center and helped me buy stationery. Since that day, I have written more than ten thousand hand-written notes — from thank-you notes to holiday cards to happy birthday notes and more.

Over the years, these principles helped me build countless genuine relationships with people who had no business spending so much time coaching a young upstart like me.

I would not be anywhere near where I am today without the support of my mentors. Compass wouldn't exist. This book wouldn't exist. None of it. But finding people who can advise and support you is much easier than most people imagine if instead of just thinking about what *you* want out of the relationship, you also think about how *they* can have a good experience mentoring you.

To recap, when you're meeting with a mentor:

- Ask for specific advice *you* can use
- Provide an insight from your world that *they* can use

- Ask personal questions that they would have fun answering
- Follow up consistently and appreciatively

The man who showed me — and so many others — that anything is possible

From poverty to the White House and beyond

As Compass's growth started taking off, I realized I was going to have to give all of my energy to the company and stop spending as much time as I had with my mentors, mentees, and non-profits.

I shared my worry with Ken Chenault, who at the time was CEO of American Express and one of the few Black CEOs of a Fortune 500 company. I told him I felt bad because he and so many others had helped me get to where I was, and since founding Compass, I'd had to put 100 percent of my focus on getting the company off the ground. I didn't want my mentors to feel that my lack of interaction was a sign that I wasn't thankful.

Ken said, "No, don't feel bad about needing to focus during this time. The best way to give back to me and those who have helped you is to make Compass very successful so you can be in a position to maximize your impact on others over your life and pass it on."

I said, "But what about Vernon?"

"Well, that's a different story," Ken replied. "You've still got to find a way to make time for Vernon. No matter what."

"Vernon" is, of course, Vernon Jordan, the only person I am close to that I still address formally: "Mr. Jordan." Every Black executive owes a debt to Vernon Jordan. He's a unique and towering figure in both business and politics who has advised more presidents and more Fortune 500 CEOs than I can count.

But he has also mentored an astonishing number of young Black people like me, and over the decades, he has become, in essence, the "rabbi" to several generations of Black professionals. In fact, most of my Black mentors consider Vernon *their* mentor. While a lot of mentors give advice, Vernon shares wisdom.

His wisdom comes from the depth and the diversity of his experiences. He was born during the Great Depression, directed the NAACP's fieldwork in Georgia during the civil rights movement, walked with Martin Luther King, ran the United Negro College Fund and the National Urban League, served as one of President Clinton's closest and most trusted advisors and led his presidential transition team, and has left a defining mark on the world of business through his work on countless corporate boards and his leadership at the investment bank Lazard, where I had the opportunity to meet, work with, and learn from him.

If you define power as how many leaders will pick up the phone if you call, Vernon Jordan is one of the most powerful people in the country.

Listening to Vernon Jordan is like listening to living history. The arcs of his stories highlight the arcs of progress in the history of the United States.

I remember when he told me that President Clinton called him the last night of his presidency and asked him to come by the White House. It was late in the evening, but Vernon came over. The two men stayed up most of the night talking and sharing old stories. Vernon then told me what it was like to drive out of the White House for what he knew would be the last time. "Robert, I stopped for a few minutes at those gates and reflected on how, for the last eight years, two poor kids from the South, one White and one Black, had led the free world together."

I teared up when he said that. It confirmed for me what I always hoped to be true: that anything was possible. Vernon was the living embodiment that nobody can prevent you from realizing your dreams.

Vernon was so good to me. He gave me advice every time I asked, invited me and my mom to Thanksgivings with his family, introduced me to several pivotal people at key moments in my life, and told me to apply for the White House Fellowship. I can still remember his smile when he told me to apply. "Robert, I believe all young professionals in the private sector should get exposure to the public sector even if for just one year because the skills you develop and the relationships you will attain will be transferable to whichever sector you choose." He then went on to say, "My good friend Colin Powell was a White House Fellow. Jeannie, can you get Colin Powell on the phone." Keep in mind, this was in late 2004 when Colin Powell was secretary of state.

There are so many words he said to me that will stay with me forever. Even now I can hear his strong, deep voice when I think of them.

I remember the first time I had a one-on-one meeting with him in his corner office on the sixty-second floor of Lazard's office in Rockefeller Center. I was a twenty-three-year-old associate at his firm, and I told him how I wanted to work for a few years then leave to start a nonprofit, and he said, "Son, you've got to make a check before you write one."

It was essentially the same advice Dick Foster had given me many years earlier when, during my first month at McKinsey, I told him about that the same goal. And it was the same guidance Henry Cornell gave me at Goldman Sachs years later. (In the end, I decided to launch a nonprofit at age twenty-nine while continuing to work so I didn't have to wait longer or give up my career.)

My second year at Lazard, I remember asking Vernon when the time would be right to take a big risk and try to do something great in public service. He said, "Son, don't leave an institution until you are one," and "Don't shoot for greatness at the expense of goodness." For years I heeded that wisdom, growing as much as I could within powerful companies and organizations. But when I decided to launch Compass with Ori, I certainly wasn't an institution and I was choosing to leave behind something good to take a chance on something great.

Vernon understood. Like all great mentors, he didn't want his advice to be followed to the letter — he wanted it to help shape my thinking. As long as I listened, took it seriously, and wrestled with the right way to apply his advice to my own life, he knew I'd find the right path. We agreed that although I wasn't an institution I had made enough of a name for myself to meet the threshold advice I had received from his mentee (and my mentor) Ray McGuire, Citigroup's global head of corporate and investment banking and perhaps the longest serving and most senior Black executive on Wall Street. Ray had told me that "Wall Street doesn't provide a revolving door. So don't leave until you have enough credibility to take a risk, fail, and get back in if it doesn't work."

In the end, Vernon gave me his blessing to start Compass. I told him I was nervous and scared that I was leaving the security of Goldman Sachs. And he then shared more words of wisdom that I will never forget. "Son, opportunity is never convenient."

I'm so grateful to Vernon for so many things. But most of all for showing me through the life he lived that Black people could be powerful and influential across all fields they touched. He carried with him the expectation that if you *could* achieve something you *would* achieve it no matter how hard you had to work to get there. He made me — and every Black professional around him — want to work really hard, not just for ourselves but to honor those who came before us and created the opportunities we had and also pave the way for those who would come after us.

Vernon made me feel like I could be as successful as I wanted to be. That may sound like a small thing, especially if you've grown up in a world that makes you feel like that all the time. But for me, it was a massive boost at a time in life where I was still looking for direction, purpose, and confidence.

Even though I knew how busy he was and how many people he mentored and advised, I always had this sense that he would somehow know if I didn't realize my full potential.

After all he'd been through and accomplished in life, I didn't want to let Vernon down. I continue to work hard each day in the hope that I never do.

What my mom and a partner at Goldman Sachs had in common

Every athlete plays harder for a great coach

Everyone needs a great coach. Someone who knows exactly how far you can push yourself because they've seen you strive and sweat and struggle. Someone you can let your guard down around because you know they're always in your corner. Someone who makes you want to be your best self, break your previous personal records, and *deliver.*

My mom was my one and only coach at first, pushing me and supporting me and cheering me on for years. As I came of age, we became collaborators, working together to plan my future and realize my dreams through countless application essays and interviews with nonprofits and schools, for scholarships and internship opportunities. When I ran fifty marathons, she became my manager and actual coach. She's one of the most competent and capable people I know and she was always my secret weapon.

The best coach in my professional career was Henry Cornell, who hired me to work in the private equity group of Goldman Sachs after I completed the White House Fellows program. Even though Henry was White, he saw himself in me. Raised in the Bronx by a single mother, he'd had to figure out for himself how to fit into a corporate world filled with the children of wealthy, well-connected families.

Henry managed me longer than any other boss I've had, and during my time with him, I grew more than I had in any previous period of my life. His advice was more perceptive than I'd ever experienced before, and while it was often blunt and hard to hear, the fact that it was so unvarnished actually made it easier for me to act on it. He was my first great corporate coach.

What made Henry stand out was how practical his advice was. For example, there was a time when a brilliant leader on our team pushed the CEO of one of our portfolio companies much too hard to adopt more rigorous standards around goal setting. My colleague kept pushing and eventually the CEO threw up his hands and quit, which is a huge risk and red flag in a newly acquired company.

Henry called in my colleague and spoke to him in an uncharacteristically loud tone. "You may be smart — in fact, you may be the smartest person in this building — but one thing you don't understand, that you will need decades of experience to understand, is that *you can be right and still lose!* You may have been right in what you did, but you lost." To this day, that's one of the top messages I share with people during the most difficult times: don't be right and lose.

Today, my primary coach is Benís. We didn't expect our relationship to unfold this way, but during the first years of Compass, when all I could think about was the company, she had a unique ability to listen and was endlessly curious about what I was going through. She never let me suffer alone even if I wanted to shield her from my worries.

Before we realized it, her counsel became so helpful that Ori could tell whether or not I had spoken to Benís about a problem based on my attitude about it. At times, she has given me the confidence to take a leap I wouldn't have had the courage to take alone, and at other times, she has helped me stand down from a battle that simply wasn't worth fighting.

I also have a terrific executive coach who I meet with regularly and we always focus on the same question: How can I be a better leader? My coach has incredible pattern recognition from his years counseling CEOs and he provides insights I couldn't spot on my own. He has accelerated my personal growth as a leader more than I could have ever imagined.

For some reason, many leaders seem to believe that asking for help, feedback, and guidance will make them appear weak. I've found just the opposite: listening to coaches has made me a much stronger leader.

When I'm able to be vulnerable and honest with wise people who have my best interests at heart, they're able to help me see my blind spots and identify the right path forward no matter how rocky the situation. What's more, the depth and fearlessness of the conversations energize me for the work ahead, giving me the spark I need to push myself to be my best self and the best leader I can be.

Before you suit up to play the game, make sure you've got a good coach to help you be your best every day.

Where I got the idea to run fifty marathons

Look for inspiration from people you respect —
and don't be afraid to follow their exact footsteps

People love the idea of coming up with something new out of thin air. Taking out a blank piece of paper and writing a masterpiece. Tinkering in your basement until you invent a better mousetrap. Writing code late at night to create the Next Big Thing.

But most great ideas don't come from geniuses working alone — and most great ideas are not entirely new or wholly original. They come from people working with other people with diverse life experiences. They come from combining familiar ingredients in new ways. They come from building on great ideas that have come before.

Think about it. If you're looking for a great idea, is it more likely you'll find it by looking inside your head or by looking at the combined creativity of tens of billions of humans over tens of thousands of years?

So how did I come up with the idea to run fifty marathons, one in each US state, to raise $1 million for nonprofits? It wasn't because I loved running so much. Or because I loved asking people I know for money. In fact, there was nothing about the fifty-marathons concept that was my original idea.

In my midtwenties, I was working nonstop and didn't have the time to do all the things that were really important to me, and I wanted to find ways to stay in better shape, spend more time with my mom, and raise money for the nonprofits that helped me when I was a student. But there simply weren't enough hours in the day.

I wanted to find some way to achieve all three goals at once. But how could I come up with an idea that would accomplish all that? I could have brainstormed big ideas on my own. I could have reached out to individual mentors to ask their advice.

Instead, I tried a different approach. I read up on all the inspiring things other people had already done to achieve similar goals. I printed out the bios of the White House Fellows from the last ten years and the Henry Crown Fellows from the Aspen Institute. I highlighted the best things I saw. Studying the bios of more than one hundred incredible people helped me learn from all of their lives in a short time. It provided me with more ideas more quickly than I could have gotten any other way.

Plus, these ideas were all *proven*. Other people had already done them, earned prestigious fellowships afterward, and deemed those achievements worthy of including in their paragraph-long bios.

One person had raised $1 million for charity by climbing the tallest mountain in North America. Someone else had completed a bicycle ride cross country with someone in his family. A third person had run fifty marathons.

I decided to bring all those ideas together into one plan. I would run fifty marathons, one in each US state, to raise $1 million for nonprofits, and I would partner with my mom and invite her to every race. The fact that I wouldn't be the *first* person to do any of these was much less relevant than their *impact.*

I combined other people's ideas to create a big dream for myself that let me rally people around a common purpose, give back to the organizations that had created opportunity in my life, get into the best shape of my life, and spend more time with my mom, who acted as my manager and attended the vast majority of the marathons. I called it Running to Support Young Dreams and managed to complete all fifty marathons in six years and support some incredible nonprofits with the $1 million we raised.

All because I took a highlighter to a bunch of bios — and chose to care more about whether the ideas had impact than whether I had invented them from scratch.

Take the right amount of risk for you
Avoid the "high-risk, high-reward" mentality

Successful CEOs often make it sound like they took these impossible risks and, amazingly enough, everything worked out great. I'm not going to do that. I want to tell you the story of how little risk I took in launching my company — and how you should try to do the same if you ever start your own business.

When I felt that my days at Goldman Sachs were drawing to an end, I started looking for my next chapter. I met with a mentor of mine, Bayo Ogunlesi, who founded the private equity firm Global Infrastructure Partners and was the lead director on the board of Goldman Sachs, to see if I could come work with him.

My goal for that meeting was to land a job. Bayo's goal for the meeting was to convince me to start my own company. We'd gotten to know each other well after he became one of the largest individual donors to New York Needs You, and he believed something that I didn't believe at all at that time: that I had what it took to found not just a nonprofit but a start-up company as well.

When I approached Bayo for a job, he gave me an assignment as part of the interview process: "Think of two great ideas of businesses you could create and present them to me. Put as much work into these ideas as you did with founding New York Needs You and let's see what comes out of it."

I didn't know why he was asking me to do what felt like a random exercise, but I assumed he wanted to assess my critical business thinking skills. So I came back a couple of months later with two ideas: a venture capital firm and a real estate rental technology start-up, both with Ori Allon, who I explained was a friend who had created one company that he sold to Google and another company that he sold to Twitter. I explained both ideas in incredible detail and outlined why the real estate business was the bigger opportunity.

Bayo said, "The real estate start-up idea sounds great. I think you should do it."

I pushed back. "Bayo, I only did this exercise because I thought it was part of the interview process for a job. I'm getting married in three months. We're going to have a kid soon. I really don't want to do this; I just want to come work for you."

He looked at me and smiled a big, slow smile — then said something that changed my life. "Look, I'll be your first investor. I'll invest $500,000, and if you fail, I'll hire you in a year." He'd been impressed enough with what he'd seen from New York Needs You to be willing to bet on me before he'd even heard a pitch. I was stunned. It's almost like I was the investment opportunity and he was pushing me to come up with something that he could invest in.

In that instant, he removed all of the risk from starting my own company. He hedged my bet and provided me with complete downside protection. That is the real story of how I "found" the courage and the confidence to start Compass: by taking zero risk. I knew that even if I failed I'd be just fine because he would hire me.

To this day, I'm amazed that he saw something in me I couldn't see. I will forever be thankful to him for how he changed my life and my family's life.

I share this story not because it makes me look particularly good or daring but because it's the true story of how someone basically forced me to take a leap that I would never have taken on my own. And I have a hunch that many more founders have stories like this that they don't often share.

It's so easy to glamorize the hardships and the risks that others have taken without knowing their full stories. And it's tempting to think that the more risk you take, the more heroic you're being. But it's not the path I took — and I know that I wouldn't have been able to create Compass if I'd thought that "high-risk, high-reward" was the only way.

THE PRINCIPLES
I LEARNED
FROM
CHILDHOOD,
MOTHERS,
AND MENTORS

Between birth and my first job after college, I learned the lessons that have shaped my life ever since.

During that time, I came to believe that everyone with a dream of a better life or a better world is an entrepreneur. Everyone is on an entrepreneurial journey at some point. Every immigrant who sets off for a foreign shore, every athlete who gives 110 percent at tryouts, everyone who's ever applied for a small-business loan — they're all aiming high even though they know they may fall short.

If you're reading this book, you're an entrepreneur — and you are capable of even more than you believe you are as long as you can dream it.

So I have distilled everything I've learned into what I believe are the eight principles of entrepreneurship.

Most of these principles *sound* simple and obvious — like something you already know. But I've come to believe that each principle is more difficult to put into practice — and more powerful once you do — than almost anyone anticipates.

The Principles of Entrepreneurship

1. **Dream big** — which I learned from my mom's own struggle for independence from her father — and which powered me through the long years of nonstop work on the way to my future

2. **Move fast** — which I learned by racing through college in two and a half years — and which helped me find my mission in life much earlier than I would have otherwise

3. **Learn from reality** — which I learned as a DJ in high school, playing whatever the customer wanted — and which helped me guide Compass's technology team to build software that helps our customers grow their business

4. **Be solutions driven** — which I learned from watching my mom adapt as a single mother and an entrepreneur — and which helped me figure out how to run my final marathon in record time

5. **Obsess about opportunity** — which I learned from the nonprofits that supported me as a high schooler — and which helped me build a relationship with the tech genius who became my cofounder at Compass

6. **Collaborate without ego** — which I learned from watching my dad suffer under the weight of feeling like he wasn't the man he was supposed to be — and which helped me create a positive, hopeful, and energetic culture at Compass

7. **Maximize your strengths** — which I learned from my very first business venture as a teenager — and which

helped me start being my best self after realizing it was possible to be your authentic self at work

8. **Bounce back with passion** — which I learned from seeing Benís fall into a depression after our second child was born then find a way to embrace life again — and which helped me navigate a major pivot at Compass that almost cost me my job

These principles have been validated and reinforced by other mentors and mothers who have guided me throughout my early career in the private, public, and nonprofit spheres; through fifty marathons; up and down on the roller-coaster of love and life; and during my most recent period founding and running Compass.

In the sections that follow, I'll try to deepen your understanding of these eight principles in the same way that I've deepened my own understanding of them over the years: through learning from the stories others have shared with me and from my own experiences trying, failing, learning, and trying again until I succeed.

My sincere hope is that each chapter leaves you with a lesson or idea that you can put into action in your own life today or tomorrow to help you realize your biggest dreams.

1

DREAM BIG

I have always found that plans are useless, but planning is indispensable.

— Dwight D. Eisenhower

Without leaps of imagination, or dreaming, we lose the excitement of possibilities. Dreaming, after all, is a form of planning.

— Gloria Steinem

Don't ever let somebody tell you you can't do something, not even me . . . If you want something, go get it. Period.

— Chris Gardner (played by Will Smith)
in *The Pursuit of Happyness*

Dream big because the world is overflowing with opportunity. Dream big because society has real problems that need fixing. Dream big because there's nothing to strive for without a dream.

Refuse to think small. Don't let long odds hold you back. Don't ask whether *something is possible, figure out* how *you will get it done.*

Big dreams generate the energy you need to succeed at anything. They stir passion, create meaning, and spur creative thinking. They call on people to do something everyone secretly yearns for: to take on an "impossible" challenge and prove everyone wrong.

Big dreams inspire others to join together in common cause. When the stakes are high and we're quenching that deep human desire to pursue something larger than ourselves, collaboration flourishes and petty conflicts recede. When you believe that anything is possible, everything becomes possible.

Entrepreneurship is inherently risky, and if the reward isn't big enough, the risk won't be worth it. But a clear and compelling vision for the future will give everyone the courage they need to leave comfort behind and leap into the unknown.

Dream big—because your ambition is the cap to your potential. The more you can dream, the more you can achieve.

Live your life like it's a movie
Every protagonist struggles at first — and ultimately triumphs

I love movies. I've learned at least as much from great movie speeches as I did from going to Columbia. Al Pacino's incredible "game of inches" speech in *Any Given Sunday.* Will Smith's character talking to his son about protecting his dreams in *The Pursuit of Happyness.* Every minute of *Rocky.*

I even try to live my own life like it's a movie. I'll tell you what I mean.

Think about a montage sequence. Filmmakers condense days

or weeks or years of tedious work and preparation into a single two-minute scene with uplifting music that propels you forward.

When I was living through periods of struggle, I actually thought of those repetitive and difficult moments as part of the montage sequence of my life.

That helped me enjoy commuting two hours each way to high school in San Francisco, regularly working until 1 a.m. through the week and at least one weekend night at a New York investment bank in my twenties, and running ten miles before work to keep in shape so I could complete a marathon in each of the fifty US states. The minutes go by faster if you allow yourself to hear that inspirational music in the background the whole time.

In a sense, I was filming the movie of my life day after day after day.

Just like any good movie, there were moments of joy, doubt, love, fear, loneliness, heartbreak, struggle, hope, betrayal, redemption, and triumph. I learned to enjoy each moment because I knew that every story *had* to have those ups and downs to be worth watching. And as every movie I've ever seen has taught me, when things seem most hopeless and impossible, it means that something truly great is likely around the corner.

Almost any experience can be filled with a heightened sense of significance when seen through the eyes of a film buff.

Picture me on a bus at 6:45 a.m. carrying a Rasta bag, a boom box, and licorice root to sell at my elite, predominantly White private high school.

Cut to me sitting alone in an office on the sixty-third floor of 30 Rockefeller Center in Manhattan, my suit rumpled after a long day, my desk illuminated by one of those old-school banker lamps with the green shade.

See the wide shot of me running along a shoreline path with the New York skyline towering above me as I prepare to raise $1 million for nonprofits by running marathons.

When I took the BART train and two buses from my home in Berkeley to my school in San Francisco each morning, I chose to see that as the opening scene of an epic journey: sunlight peeking over the tops of buildings while suit-wearing professionals filled with intense purpose traveled to do what I imagined was exciting work in one of the coolest cities in the world.

There are, of course, other ways to view that same scene. Haggard commuters dragging themselves into work in some lifeless office very early in the morning could have been a signal of the drudgery ahead in adult life. But adding substance, meaning, and glory to the scene, seeing the light rather than imagining the darkness, viewing it as a journey rather than a commute — all of that helped me start each day filled with dreams and possibility.

Living my life through this cinematic lens inspired me to advance the plot of my life. Something exciting always happens in movies, so if my life is a movie, something *had* to happen for me, too. And as the protagonist in my own story, I knew it was up to me to make something happen.

What's more, I had to move fast because I didn't have much time. A great film can tell an epic story that spans a lifetime in just ninety minutes. A movie trailer boils that down into just three fast-paced, high-energy minutes.

Meanwhile, the rest of us live each day of our lives minute by minute and hour by hour. In three minutes, we manage to live . . . three minutes.

Human memory functions more like the movies than our daily experiences. When we're looking backward, we remember only the biggest triumphs, the most meaningful interactions, the most difficult struggles — and let everything else fade away.

I try to do that in real time. To look at myself through a new lens. To put the mundanity and struggle into context. To add a larger, bolder arc to my own narrative even as I'm living it.

Make decisions you'll be proud of when you're old
An important goal of life is to be content in your rocking chair

When you're in the middle of a complicated situation — deep in the details and the trade-offs — it can sometimes be hard to see the right path forward.

I've found it helpful in those moments to imagine myself looking back at the decision from the future. From that distant vantage point, what would I feel about the decision I'm making today?

It's remarkably clarifying. And it works better the more vividly you imagine your future self and the more seriously you take it.

I've developed a very clear picture of myself in, say, the year 2050: Benís and I are living in the beautiful city of San Diego and enjoying its perfect weather and gorgeous ocean views. I'm seventy-one years old, sitting in a rocking chair on our porch, looking out at the water and reminiscing. I might be drinking some lemonade. Most important, I have no regrets.

This exercise — which I call the "rocking chair test" — has led me to a few realizations.

The most important factor in my happiness is my family. When I imagine a future where I've accomplished more than I ever dreamed — but ended up divorced from my wife and estranged from my children — it's a million times worse than when I imagine

accomplishing absolutely nothing except nurturing my closest relationships and earning my family's love.

**Decades from now, I won't even remember most of the de-
cisions I'm making right now.** I make multiple tough calls every
single day, but when I think back, I can recall only a handful of
decisions that I made last year. It's liberating to realize just how
much our brains inflate the importance of the things right in
front of us when most "big deals" aren't very big at all.

**The decisions I'll remember most are the ones I'm either
proud of or regret.** If no answer seems totally right in the present, I tend to choose the one I know I'm least likely to regret. And
if I can tell that one of the paths is the right thing to do even if it's
going to make some people angry, I work hard to find the courage to do it. Because I know that the more moments of pride I
create in my life, the more content I'll be in that rocking chair.

Over the last few years, the choices that have been toughest have generally been around difficult HR decisions—letting
someone go who I like personally but know isn't right for the role
—or moments when our country feels like it's faced with a moral
reckoning and I feel moved to speak out.

It can be hard since, as a business leader, I represent people
with very different views. I cherish our country's history of open
debate and I don't want to make anyone who works at Compass
feel like they don't belong. But in cases like President Trump's executive order in early 2017 barring entry into the United States
by people from certain countries with Muslim-majority popu-
lations, often called the "Muslim ban," the White supremacist
and neo-Nazi rally that took place in Charlottesville, Virginia,
in August 2017, the separation of immigrant children from their
families at the border, and the murder of George Floyd by Min-

neapolis police in 2020, I chose to share my personal views with the entire Compass community and the public.

When I'm in that rocking chair in thirty years, I'm pretty sure I'll be proud of those decisions to speak up.

TWENTY-TWO ITEMS FROM THE BUCKET LIST I WROTE AT AGE TWENTY-TWO

When I was having a hard time getting over the breakup with my college sweetheart, I decided to dream my way out of the pain by envisioning a positive future. So I wrote down my Top One Hundred Lifelong Ambitions and Experiences. Under the heading Objective of List, I wrote: "To be used as a reminder of who I am at the core when life gets too hectic and the world is too overwhelming."

Here are my top ten life goals from that list.

1. Marry an intelligent, honest, imaginative, creative, driven, hopelessly romantic, curious, selfless, joyful, patient, demanding, loyal, supportive, funny, charismatic, affectionate, thoughtful, spontaneous, adaptable, attentive, supportive, centered, reliable, dependable, emotionally stable, kind, challenging, magical, confident woman who will run with me, treats everyone the same, is my best friend, has a deep desire to be an amazing mother, can talk about her emotions, is comfortable in every environment and at peace with her place in the world yet still ambitious, is a true partner in every way, cuddles with me, camps with me, loves me for who I am at the core, and who makes me want to be a better man
2. Earn the love and respect of my children

3. Grow to be completely comfortable in my own skin
4. Find a profession that represents the best and highest use of myself
5. Learn to make bad events/conflict/competition make me better and not bitter
6. Be the best husband, father, and friend that I can be
7. Have a cartoon that I watch with my kids religiously every Saturday
8. Play with my grandchildren and tell them my life story while they get bored listening to it for the tenth time
9. Raise my kids to be confident, curious, centered, and content (the rest will follow)
10. Talk to my mother, children, and wife every day

And here are some entries from the rest of the list (which ended up being 105 items long).

21. Motorcycle across Latin America (north to south)
24. Open for a reggae/rock concert saying, "Are you ready" . . . and the audience says "YEEAAHH"
39. Write an autobiography called *Search for the Sparkle*, and a book of advice to pass along to the next generation
44. Become the CEO of a Fortune 500 company
62. Save someone's life
64. Take my kids to the soup kitchen every holiday season to show them the diversity of the world they live in
68. Study the Seven Wonders of the Ancient World and visit the Seven Wonders of the Modern World
73. Get to a point in my life, emotionally or financially, where I don't care about money
81. Call the president of the United States to advocate for

something that improves quality of life for millions of people

83. Understand what it takes to be truly happy
96. Drink from spring water that I am swimming in
105. Die at home in my sleep surrounded by friends and family after having a good life, and after I pass, have my ashes mixed with my wife's ashes and planted in the ground with a seed of the biggest and most beautiful long-living tree so our love continues to grow and be intertwined for generations to come

Twenty years later, I've made some progress — but I have a whole lot more to do in the decades to come. I can't wait.

The dream that seemed too big

What I learned from the younger generation of Black activists

It didn't take me long after I got to New York City for me to realize that while it was arguably the most diverse city in the world it was also one of the most segregated.

Police would stop me and my Black friends in the street when we hadn't done anything wrong, which never happened to my White friends.

Bouncers wouldn't let me into clubs, saying that I was wearing sneakers or jeans or a shirt without a collar even as they let my White friends in who were dressed the same as I was.

Taxi drivers drove right past me as I stood on the curb with my hand raised only to pick up a White passenger farther down the block.

These things didn't happen just once or twice — they happened more than a hundred times.

I was hurt. I was humiliated. And I was angry.

I didn't think I could change racism. I considered it a fact of life, so I tried not to think about the unfairness of it and decided to "work twice as hard," as so many of my Black mentors told me to do. I suppressed my emotions and channeled them into making it impossible for people to hold me back.

I wasn't going to let anybody tell me what I could or could not be. I wasn't going to let anyone else define me. I wasn't going to let anyone stop me from living my dreams.

For two decades, because of the type of person that I am, that approach worked fairly well for me. No, it wasn't always easy, but I was so focused on not being consumed by negativity that I learned to keep moving no matter what.

Then George Floyd was murdered by police in Minneapolis and the entire country saw that heartbreaking video.

The protests that sprung up across the nation and the world, and the moral reckoning that followed, were unlike anything I'd ever seen in my life. For the first time, it felt like non-Black people finally saw that there was real racism in the world, that they genuinely cared about the suffering of Black people, and that they wanted to do something about it.

Millions of people across the country were learning, some for the first time, just how much anti-Black racism and bias and discrimination there was in our country. And many Black and brown folks were going through the painful process of reliving trauma and remembering everything they'd experienced in their lives that for many was bottled up inside.

I did some difficult soul-searching in those weeks and learned something powerful about myself and the long arc of progress.

Despite all those times my mom had told me to have big dreams, I'd actually learned *not* to dream very big about racial equity in America. My mentors told me over and over again that the opportunities I was given in life were thanks to the sacrifices of Black people who came before me and that it was my responsibility to work hard, prove myself, "fit in," and make sure the doors would stay open for the next generation.

But in the spring of 2020, I learned that the younger thinkers and activists who were leading the movement for justice had internalized a completely different message.

As the LGBTQ+ nonprofit leader Eliza Byard said to me in a fireside chat that we livestreamed to our company during the protests, "One thing that gives me hope is that there are a couple of generations of children, teenagers, and young adults who *expect* to be included. They won't have it any other way."

It took me a minute to take that in.

I'd never heard that message from my mentors or peers.

I'd never had that expectation of the world.

I'd never let myself dream that big.

But these young people *had,* and because of their big dreams, they are changing America and they are changing the world. There is still, of course, so much more to be done, but what they accomplished in 2020 was possible because of the scope of their ambitions. As my friend and fellow Black CEO Wes Moore has said, "We are not the products of our environments, we are the products of our expectations."

The expectation of equality from so many young people today has taught me to dream big once again. And I'll be forever grateful to them for that.

2

MOVE FAST

I'd rather regret the things I've done than regret the things I haven't done.

—Lucille Ball

It's been my observation that most people get ahead during the time that others waste.

—Henry Ford

You can't be that kid standing at the top of the waterslide, overthinking it. You have to go down the chute.

—Tina Fey

Move fast to see your ideas come to life as soon as possible.
   Move fast because you have limited resources and too much to do in too little time.

Move fast because you're passionate and driven, and the faster you move, the more energy you create in the world.

Move fast because I've never once met a customer who wanted their question answered or their problem solved more slowly. *Speed conveys care to your customers.*

Move fast because if a problem is actually as big as it seems, you won't be the only person who sees it — but if you move fast, you might be the first person to solve it.

But most of all, move fast because you need to learn *fast. The greatest advantage you have in life is the speed at which you learn, so you have to learn fast. Moving fast is about going from* not knowing to knowing *as quickly as possible.*

Nothing is real until the ideas in an entrepreneur's head come into contact with the world. Real customers are the only way to discover that a design is a dud or turn a hunch into a hit. The faster you can go from not understanding to understanding, the likelier it is you'll succeed — regardless of whether your customers' initial reactions are positive or negative.

These principles are all related: Once you have big dreams, you need to move fast so you can learn from reality.

Focus on results, not activities

Success only comes from delivering measurable impact

Everyone in business thinks they're too busy. It's practically right there in the word itself: busyness. But most people, most of the time, might be less busy if they weren't focused on the wrong things.

At Compass, after spinning our wheels on too many projects for too long, we've started to focus on results — and results *only.*

Not hard work and long hours. Not activity. Not effort. Not meetings. Not marketing campaigns. Not product launches.

Just results.

Results are measurable and can clearly show if you were successful or not. Everything else may or may not have any impact.

In the early years at Compass, I started to notice that people felt good about their work when they were working hard and completing projects — even if the project wasn't ultimately driving success for our customers or the company. Moving us away from an activity-based culture to a results-based culture was one of the most important things we ever did.

Let me illustrate what I mean.

A while back, a number of Compass real estate agents told us they wanted a world-class presentation to give to potential clients who were planning to sell their homes. These meetings, called listing presentations, are one of the main ways that agents win new business, so getting them right can have an outsize, positive effect.

If we had an *activity*-based culture, we might have thought we were successful if we'd created and distributed a new presentation, on schedule, with different options and choices and held a training session on how to use it. And if we had sent out a feedback survey afterward, we would have probably felt like we'd knocked that project out of the park. But we would have only been holding ourselves accountable to getting the listing presentation done, not to ensuring that the listing presentation helped agents win more business.

Since we're building a *results*-based culture, however, we wanted to know *far* more than that. We wanted to know that our efforts had actually been measurably and verifiably successful at driving better outcomes for our agents. Otherwise, how would we know that all that work had been worth doing in the first place?

Rather than being satisfied with simply launching a new presentation on time, we wanted to be able to say that the agents who were using the new listing presentation were winning 50 percent more listings than agents using the old one.

Rather than just holding a training session, we wanted to know that the trainings were widely attended — and that 90 percent of the people who received the training felt that it helped them grow their business.

Rather than just emailing people a survey, we wanted to gather fine-grained feedback on how to make the next version even stronger, have agents pinpoint the highest-impact changes, then rush to get a new and improved version into agents' hands as quickly as possible.

People often find excuses to not focus on results for good reason: you might not hit your goals. And let's face it, it's much easier to prove that you're doing a lot of work than it is to show that you're having a lot of measurable impact.

But don't let that fear convince you to seek comfort by simply staying busy. Don't fall for the trap of feeling good about working hard on a lot of different things. Driving real results is the only way to create progress — and nothing is more satisfying or fulfilling than progress.

To achieve true balance, integrate work and life
Nothing says "romance" like a networking brunch

When I was in my late twenties and early thirties, it felt like I was constantly being put in touch with someone new who was either asking for help or who wanted to help me, but between work and marathon training, I didn't have enough time to meet them.

My solution was to host an ongoing series of large networking brunches where I could connect with these people and also create a space for them to connect with one another.

For several years, I hosted a brunch for about fifty people almost every other weekend — and sometimes two times in a single weekend even though I went to the office before and after each event. Given my personal and professional background, the get-togethers alternated between the Private Sector Peers Brunch for Black professionals and the Private Sector Backgrounds with Public Sector Interests Brunch. More than five hundred different people attended these brunches.

By combining social connection and professional networking, and finding a way to do it at such a large scale, I was able to develop and maintain relationships with significantly more people than I'd ever have been able to meet with on a one-on-one basis.

So many good things came out of the brunches. In fact, my second date with Benís was at one of them! Part of me cringes a little when I admit that, but it actually worked for both of us. I'd already taken her out on a very nice first date: dinner at Cafe Noir followed by *In the Heights,* Lin-Manuel Miranda's musical about the Dominican American neighborhood of Washington Heights in New York City (and Benís was Dominican!), followed by live music at the Groove in the Village, a friend's thirtieth birthday party, and dancing at one of her favorite spots near NYU.

Inviting her on a second date at a networking brunch was a way to find time to be with her while also introducing her to part of my world — and, in the process, revealing a *lot* about the type of person I am.

Six years later, after Benís and I were married and had just become parents and I was training for my fiftieth marathon, I found another way to integrate multiple parts of my life. I invited Benís to bring Raia down to the track so they could watch me train and we could have some fun talking in between laps. Then Benís decided to start training with me, and we asked Elida to come down with Raia and watch. In so doing, we managed to combine *four* activities into one outing: exercise for both of us, outside time for Raia, grandparent time with Elida, and family time for our new little family.

My desire to accomplish multiple goals at once was part of my rationale for running fifty marathons in the first place: getting in shape, giving back to the community, traveling the country, and spending time with my mom.

To be clear, I don't believe in doing multiple things at the same time. That's multitasking, which has been shown to be ineffective. What I've found helpful is to do a single thing that accomplishes multiple *goals*.

Now that Compass serves more than 20,000 real estate agents, I've been able to see that this lesson holds across large groups of people in widely different circumstances. I've noticed that the agents who are happiest aren't the ones who strictly separate work and life — they are the ones who are able to integrate work and life gracefully. The people who can leave the office to pick their kids up every day after school but also feel just fine bringing their kids to their open houses on the weekend.

What I've learned from watching these small-business owners is that you're still the same person whether you're doing work or living life — and you may be able to get more done and feel more fulfilled if you allow yourself to be your *full* self more of the time.

Getting out is as important as getting in
The day I realized my days were numbered at Goldman Sachs

I had the same nightmare hundreds of times in my twenties and thirties.

I'm in the office of whatever job I had at the time, but I'm wandering the halls all alone. I have this sickening, sinking feeling in my stomach that tells me it's all over. That everything I've built or achieved in my life is suddenly gone. That I'm going to lose my job, and my reputation, and all my savings, and not be able to provide for my kids or my wife or my mom. I'm wracking my brain for how to get out of the situation, but my sense of dread is telling me I'm about to lose everything.

Part of it is classic impostor syndrome — the feeling that everyone else is going to one day realize that you're a fraud.

Part of it, I'm sure, is the result of being abandoned by my grandparents and father, and watching my mom go through good years and bad years in business when I was young, and even watching her go bankrupt once.

Part of it was that, in the world of finance, once you're out, you're out. You do not get invited back in. I saw this happen to other people many times.

And part of it comes from a healthy urge to always think ahead and line up my next chapter in life so I'm never caught off-guard and always have an exit strategy ready to go.

In college, that exit strategy was a job in consulting at McKinsey, which I landed despite my bad grades.

At McKinsey, the exit strategy was going to business school.

At Lazard, the exit strategy was the White House Fellowship.

But after the White House, I got my dream job at the time at Goldman Sachs. Rather than doing two years here and two years there, I ended up staying for three years, then four, then five. As I moved from role to role, I created exit strategies within the same firm so my résumé would look more consistent, and I eventually became chief of staff to the president and chief operating officer, Gary Cohn. It was a great run, but I could tell I wasn't doing as well as required to ultimately thrive at Goldman Sachs. Yes, I would *survive*, but I would never thrive.

Still, I felt relatively secure. Until I didn't.

I remember vividly that fateful day when my nightmare came to life. Gary Cohn and I were on a plane in Japan, ready to fly home. One of our meetings had gone long and I'd gotten us to the airfield later than we'd originally planned. After we'd settled in and buckled up, the pilot came out of the cockpit with an unhappy look on his face, walked back to us, and said that we couldn't take off because we were a few minutes past the last allowable departure time. Even though we were flying on a private plane, we were still subject to aviation guidelines.

It doesn't matter if it was my fault or not; when working at that level of a company, it's *always* your fault. The bottom line was that Gary wasn't going to be able to fly home in time to see his kids as planned.

I could see in his eyes that he had lost trust in me in a way that wasn't going to be repairable for a role like chief of staff. Gary wasn't the sort to fire me on the spot or anything, but I knew I needed an exit strategy from Goldman as soon as possible.

For the record, I don't blame Gary Cohn for his reaction one bit. Now that I'm a CEO, I know how heartbreaking it is to have to call my kids up from a work trip to tell them it's going to be even longer until I can see them next. In fact, after a particularly intense year at Compass, my daughter Raia made me promise her that I wouldn't miss bedtime more than two days per week for the entire next year — and for fifty of fifty-two weeks, I kept my promise. If someone on my team made a mistake that caused me to miss bedtime for another night, I would be just as frustrated as Gary was.

While that day at the airport in Japan helped me relearn my lesson about always thinking about what's next, it also led directly to the only period in my life where I *haven't* been planning my next move. My search for a new job after Goldman ironically led to the greatest professional period in my life: Compass, where I discovered that one of the best parts of building something yourself is that you can pour all of your energy and passion into it without having to spend time lining up backup plans. While always envisioning my exit strategy was essential throughout my career, I've found that the only way for me to be truly successful as an entrepreneur is to let go of that Plan B mindset and go all in.

Find small things that make a big difference

The phone call I make dozens of times each week

Now that Compass is a multibillion-dollar company, you might think that the best way for me to be influential is to raise money, set strategy, and make tough judgment calls.

Even though I make decisions all the time that affect hundreds or even thousands of people, it's the one-on-one interactions that make the biggest difference.

The most valuable thing I do as CEO of Compass — on a per-minute basis — is call every employee and agent team leader who has agreed to join the company. I welcome them to the Compass family and let them know that I am excited to have them on the team and that I look forward to getting to know them. I know how it feels to start at a new company and know how meaningful it would have been for me to have the CEO reach out, so it has always felt like the right thing to do.

The calls go something like this:

Hey, it's Robert Reffkin, the CEO of Compass. I heard the great news about tomorrow. I wanted to call you in advance and welcome you formally to the Compass family. I'll come by tomorrow and say "Hi" in person [which I do during their onboarding]. *But I just wanted to welcome you to Compass. I'm really glad to have you on the team.* Sometimes I'll add, *I saw that you came from* [Apple], *there are a lot of great people who've come from* [Apple] *here. I know you're going to do great things and I'm really looking forward to getting to know you.*

The calls last less than a minute each and less than 10 percent of folks pick up, so they're mostly in the form of voice mails. But the impact they have is greater than you'd ever believe.

It's not that my message is so special — it's that I'm the CEO of the company they just started working for and I'm taking the time to reach out.

Joining a new organization is incredibly stressful. You're wondering, on your first day, whether you belong. Whether people know that you're there. Whether they care. Having someone notice you and welcome you helps you succeed. *No one succeeds alone.*

The calls are meaningful to me, too. Because I regularly make twenty of these calls in a single day, I'm constantly thinking about the new people we're bringing into the company. It's easy for leaders to get complacent and turn their attention inward; these calls keep me focused on what it's like on day one at Compass.

I didn't expect that people would react to these calls in the way they do, and it took me a while to figure out why they meant so much to folks. But one thing about me is that when I find something that works I keep doing it until it stops working.

For a long time, people have been expecting that I'll stop making these welcome calls. Maybe when we've hired one hundred people? Or five hundred? Or one thousand? Or ten thousand? But I'm still going. If a small action can have a large impact, why *wouldn't* you keep doing it?

Enjoy moments of pure happiness when they come
Three golden memories of my journey to New York City

Moving fast is essential to success. But even as you're moving fast, you have to remember to take a breath and savor a moment of joy sometimes.

For a person like me who spends so much time dreaming about the future and so little time noticing the present, this has been a difficult lesson to learn and an even harder lesson to put into practice.

I've let so many good moments in my life fly by without marking or celebrating them — many of which I can now hardly recall at all. The day I was accepted into a private high school. The day I was hired at McKinsey. The day we officially launched Compass. I know they were meaningful moments, but I didn't take a second to let them sink in. I immediately focused on the next task, the next problem to solve, the next dream.

But that being said, there have been a number of times in my life when I've gotten it right for whatever reason.

I vividly remember getting that letter from Columbia University telling me I'd been accepted. I sat there with my mom, both of us in tears, staring at the acceptance letter and the pictures of students studying on the steps of Low Memorial Library next to the Alma Mater statue. I remember that feeling vividly: that anything is possible. I felt like Charlie in *Charlie and the Chocolate Factory;* my acceptance letter was my golden ticket to make any big dream come true.

But I managed to enjoy the feeling of holding that letter in my hands and the joyful sensation it created in my heart that day.

The same was true six months later when I was driving cross-country from Berkeley all the way to New York City with my mom and my high school girlfriend, Eyla. That trip — which was quite long and quite short at the same time — provided an abundance of moments for reflection, anticipation, and excitement. Every hour, I was getting closer to my future. Every minute, I was getting the opportunity to see another part of our vast country. Every second, I was with people I loved and who loved me.

But the purest happiness came my first night in New York City after I'd moved into my dorm and said goodbye to Eyla and my mom, and I was fully on my own in the greatest city in the world. I went down to Times Square in the evening and stayed there until four in the morning, watching the lights and the people and feeling the rhythm of the city. It felt like I'd made it and that anything was possible. I don't think I've ever enjoyed a good feeling for a longer uninterrupted time than I did that night.

A mentor once said that being a start-up founder feels like you are hiking up a hill, and every time you get to what you *think* is the peak, you realize that there is a bigger hill still ahead.

He wasn't wrong. But if I take the time at the end of each day to turn around and look out over the glorious landscape I've just trekked across and truly appreciate its beauty, it gives me the energy to wake up the next day and travel higher.

Once I learned to see it that way, I realized that slowing down to appreciate a moment is *not* failing to move fast — it's actually necessary in order to be able to *keep* moving fast day after day after day.

3

LEARN FROM REALITY

You will only fail to learn if you do not learn from failing.

—Stella Adler

Those who do not want to imitate anything produce nothing.

—Salvador Dalí

If I have seen further, it is by standing on the shoulders of giants.

—Isaac Newton

The greatest advantage you have in life is the speed at which you learn—so you have to learn fast.

One of the best places to learn is from your customers. Learn everything you possibly can from the people you serve.

Think of the restaurant owner who gets to know the regulars. The DJ who watches carefully for which tracks keep people dancing. The mayor who reads the mail from her constituents every day. The software engineer who builds a survey into their app to get more feedback. The teacher who asks students about what's going on at home.

The fastest way to learn is to learn from reality.

That means studying what's come before, observing what's working right now, asking customers what they want in the future, and quickly testing new ideas to gather real reactions. It means being genuinely curious, nondefensive, and open-minded.

You can save hours and weeks and years by learning from reality rather than trying to invent everything from scratch. It's the key to doing hard things the easy way — but that doesn't mean it's easy.

Learning from reality takes humility. You have to show respect to the people who came before by looking for the brilliance in their ideas rather than pointing out the shortcomings.

It takes curiosity. You have to seek out ideas, insights, and inspiration from everyone you interact with.

It takes courage. You have to share your ideas before they're "ready," watch them fail, and learn from the experience.

And it takes strength. You have to open your ears and your heart to critical feedback in order to truly learn.

But learning from reality makes it possible to change reality for the better.

How to make the biggest decision in your life
Three ways I knew that Benís was the one for me, and one way she knew I was right for her

The question that I asked my mentors the most often in my twenties is also the most important question any of us ever ask: How do you know when you're with the right person and it's time to get married?

If I hadn't gotten such good advice, I might not be married to my wonderful wife today. I have so many single male friends who seem to have let their ego and their desire for perfection keep them from making a commitment.

The "have you been happy?" test

The first bit of wisdom came from my mentor Ken Chenault. I'd visit him about once a year at the executive suite of the American Express Tower in Manhattan, which has the most incredible views of New York Harbor.

Like many remarkable leaders, Ken has the ability to radically simplify complex issues. Marriage was no different. He thought that most men overcomplicated the question by focusing on whether they were at the right point in their career, whether they would be able to provide sufficiently, and whether they would have regrets.

Ken has a more direct approach. He said, "I'm just going to ask you one question: Over the three years you've shared with Benís, have you been happy?" And I responded, "Yes, I have been happy." Then he said, "If you have been happy, you're likely to keep being happy once you're married."

He was basically telling me to learn from reality — to focus on what had actually happened in real life rather than trying to imagine what *might* happen. And it worked. When I thought back, I realized that I had been unusually happy during our time together, and while we've had our ups and downs in marriage like all couples, our downs have brought us closer and made us stronger. I've continued to be unusually happy overall ever since.

The "wait until you're thirty" rule

The second piece of advice came from Dick Foster, who was a partner at McKinsey for decades. He said: "Wait until you're thirty or want to have kids to get married." His view was that you're still growing as a person before then. If you get married earlier, you're taking on unnecessary risk, making a bet that you'll both like the ways the other changes during those tumultuous years of finding your place in the world. Each year you wait, you're learning more about yourself, which makes it easier to know who you are and who the person you're marrying is.

In my case, I did both. I was thirty-three years old when I proposed, and I asked Benís if she was ready to have kids as soon as she stopped crying with joy. (That last part I would not recommend to others. Benís teases me about it to this day.) We ended up compromising a bit on the timeline and our first daughter was born about a year later.

And while we've both changed since, and will certainly change more in the future, the cores of our identities and personalities were set enough to know that we were a good match from the start.

The acceptance test

I've been in many relationships with women who wanted to change me — and I realize that I sometimes have tried to change the women I'm with as well. While I think we should all grow and change constantly in our lives, I've come to believe that the only way that can happen in a relationship is if you start from a place of total acceptance and love — a lesson I learned from Benís. That doesn't mean they have to like everything about you, it just means they have to accept you and love you for you, not for who they think you might become.

So ask yourself, *Does this person accept me for who I am, or are they trying to change me?* If they do accept you, and you feel the same way about them, I recommend putting a ring on that person's finger without delay.

The 80 percent rule

The perfect person for you won't be perfect themselves. Because nobody's perfect. (And if you think you're the exception to that rule, I'm willing to bet that you're still single.)

Benís and I have come up with a rule that we share whenever anyone asks for advice on these matters: If a person has 80 percent of what you're looking for, don't worry about the other 20 percent.

Since we've been married, we've seen lots of friends stay single because they're holding out for someone who checks 100 percent of their boxes. They find people with 80 percent of the qualities they want in a life partner but focus too much on the 20 percent that's not right instead of the 80 percent that is. They end those relationships in search of that missing 20 percent only to find that their new boyfriend or girlfriend has a different set of downsides.

If you make peace with the fact that we're all imperfect before you get married, it allows you to celebrate what's wonderful in your partner without dwelling on what's not.

I hope these rules help you as much as they have helped me. And I hope you find someone as singularly amazing for you — or at least as happy-making, accepting, and 80 percent right — as Benís has been for me. Because of all the decisions we make in life — where to live, where to go to school, what job to pursue — none is more important than deciding which person to spend your life with.

Watch people's faces when you talk
Why I rehearse some speeches one hundred times

Whenever you're talking to someone in a business context, you probably have some sort of goal or objective: helping them or asking for help, inspiring them or getting inspired, hiring them or convincing them to hire you.

One thing is certain: if you don't capture their attention right away, you won't achieve your goal. And if you don't keep them engaged, nothing's going to come out of the conversation. This was true when I was applying for scholarships, interviewing for jobs, and meeting with mentors, and it's true today when I am recruiting agents and employees, meeting with investors, and sharing our vision to inspire people internally and externally.

That's why I look closely at people's faces when I talk to them. I study their eyes for small shifts in interest. I look to their mouths and expressions for signs of passion, curiosity, or boredom. Do they look tired or excited? Are they leaning in or leaning back? Do they look like they want to build on what I'm saying or are they looking to get out of the conversation?

When I notice that a particular message I'm trying to convey isn't landing, I switch to another. When hiring real estate agents, I can talk about our culture and values, how our marketing can help build their brand, how our technology can save them time, or all the ways we'll help them grow their business. The faster I can determine which of those points is most meaningful to the person sitting across the table, the more likely I am to succeed in recruiting them. This is learning from reality at its finest.

When I speak to a larger group, their reactions matter just as much to me. Not out of vanity or ego but out of a desire to accomplish my goals and not waste their time. If the words I'm saying are not actually making people feel something, what's the point? They won't remember any of the ideas and the overall experience won't motivate them going forward. That's why I rehearse some speeches more than one hundred times with small groups of people and watch their faces closely before I actually deliver the final speech. I make major changes to my presentation throughout this process, overhauling the structure if it's not working and throwing away lines I love if they don't connect with other people. I want to make sure that every single point lands with real impact.

I think I first learned how to adapt based on people's responses when I was a DJ in high school. If people weren't excited by a particular song, I had just a few moments to switch things up or they'd leave the dance floor. And I learned that it was much harder to get someone moving again once they'd walked away than it was to make a quick change and keep them moving.

When talking to someone, it's too easy to get wrapped up in the question, *Am I saying what I want to say?* rather than asking the more important questions: *Is the other person hearing me? Am I connecting with them? Do their eyes look engaged?* If not, it's time to change things up — fast.

Be humble enough to learn from everyone
If millions of people told you something, would you listen?

Entrepreneurs need to be scrappy problem-solvers to figure out how to compete with larger, better-funded organizations. And entrepreneurs need to be excellent listeners to figure out what their potential customers really want and need.

For both of those reasons, entrepreneurs should constantly study what well-established companies have done before — and what competing companies are doing right now. It is, quite clearly, the fastest way to learn.

Yet, when I share this philosophy, people often don't like it. They say something along the lines of "But I don't want to *copy*, I want to *innovate*." I have two responses to that.

1. **Most innovation is integration — not invention.** Take something like the iPod, a game-changing product from the company consistently rated the most innovative in the world. But Apple didn't invent the idea of a portable MP3 player. Apple didn't invent the tiny hard drive inside. Apple didn't invent the idea of downloading individual songs instead of albums. It didn't invent the idea of white earbud headphones. But it did combine them all in an entirely new way to deliver an exceptional experience for hundreds of millions of consumers. When integration is done right, as Apple has demonstrated, it feels much more revolutionary than something "new" that fails to amaze and delight customers.

2. **Pure invention is important — but only if it's truly necessary.** Entrepreneurs, especially in the start-up world, often want to start from scratch. A blank page. First principles. Inspiration-and-caffeine-powered late-night coding sessions to turn an idea into a prototype. We all know the stories of when that has worked and a single person's spark lit the world on fire. But you hear less about the hundreds of thousands of solo efforts that go nowhere. The truth is, trying to create from whole cloth like that is incredibly risky and highly unlikely to work.

And yet I talk to people every week who choose to disregard everything that came before and completely dismiss the work of their competitors.

Even if you believe legacy companies are doing it wrong and need to be disrupted, and even if you believe you're going to solve the problem so much better than any of your competitors, don't you still want to know *what they're doing* so you can learn from it?

To arrive at the conclusion that you have nothing to learn from *anyone,* you have to think that *so* many other people at *so* many other companies are doing *absolutely everything wrong.* But is every software engineer at a rival firm misguided? Of course not. Are the millions of customers visiting a competitor's website delusional? Not a chance. Is every CEO who makes a different strategic decision than you clueless? Nope.

I don't like to say anything negative about anyone, but I can't help but feel that this is a terribly arrogant line of thinking. You're putting your own ego — I am the only one smart enough to do anything right — over the needs of your customers, many of whom are also actively using these rival services.

At Compass, we compete intensely with other real estate technology companies like Zillow, Redfin, and Opendoor as well as local and regional brokerage firms across the nation. I strongly believe in Compass's mission, vision, and strategy. I think we've got the best approach and the highest chances of success. But that being said, I also think we have really worthy and intelligent competitors who are making reasonable choices and doing tons of things right. We can all learn from one another.

I find it useful to look at what our competitors are building and ask myself, *What problems are they prioritizing and why? What must they be hearing from their customers? What can we learn from how they're approaching these issues that will help us serve our agents, buyers, and sellers better?*

I ask all employees to start any project by studying everything else that's out there by not only seeing what the trends are or what's popular but also asking themselves *why* they think those ideas might have been *good* ideas. If we want to build something differently, we should ask ourselves why we think our way is better than the current solution that's already being used by millions of people.

It all comes from a simple philosophy.

- Start from humility, not grandiosity
- Learn everything you can from everyone you can
- Integrate the best existing ideas to serve your customers, not your ego
- And then — and *only* then — look for gaps and opportunities to innovate

Having done everything you can the easy way, you'll have saved your energy, brilliance, creativity, and resources for when the only way to solve a problem for your customers is by creating something brand-new.

Ask customers what they need — and *listen* when they answer

The most important piece of technology we've built was also the simplest

I remember the day that the team at Compass showed me a preview version of a tool we now call the Customer Feedback Forum as part of a longer presentation of various software projects in development. They told me it was launching in the next month or so.

I said, "No, let's launch it tomorrow." We ended up compromising and launching it a few days later. *Move fast.*

Technically, the Customer Feedback Forum is very simple. But it's had a transformative impact on our company.

It allows any agent to suggest an idea for something new for us to build, offer, or do — and then vote on their favorite ideas from other agents. There's no fancy algorithm, no dazzling visual design, no artificial intelligence. Just a simple form where you can submit something and a simple way to make the most popular ideas rise to the top.

At first, it was designed for technology and software ideas only. But we quickly expanded it to more categories. Marketing. Community and culture. Ideas to grow your business. Training. New cities and regions. Office space. Support.

There was pushback, to be sure.

Do we really want feedback on all those things?

Do we really want to create an open forum for anyone in the company to tell us what we're doing wrong?

My answer was unequivocal: yes and yes.

Once the ideas started flowing in, there was often hesitation to embrace the ideas. Sometimes people thought the ideas were too basic to be useful. They thought a certain feature suggestion didn't leverage our technology expertise enough to be worth our time to build. They thought the simplifications weren't necessary or possible.

Since we launched the Customer Feedback Forum, though, the vast majority of our best ideas have come directly from submissions. Not because our employees aren't brilliant and creative but because our customers understand what they want better than anyone else ever could. When you're building for a particular customer — in our case, real estate agents — the only thing that matters is what *they* want.

Learning from reality is the fastest way to learn; anything that can help us learn from reality faster is worth its weight in gold.

But instead of being excited to learn, many people let fear creep in. What's worse, they are afraid of the *wrong things.*

Don't be afraid of your customers making you look bad by

saying that something's not working. Be worried about something *not* working and nobody telling you.

Don't be afraid of people thinking you're unoriginal because you're only building what your customers told you to. Be worried about wasting time building things that *don't actually help* your customers.

Don't be afraid of being buried by so much feedback that it's hard to get through your inbox. Be worried about being out of touch and losing your connection to your customers.

I've learned these lessons the hard way. We have spent thousands of hours and tens of millions of dollars building things our customer didn't end up wanting — all because we got excited about an idea we came up with that hadn't come from our customers. In all honesty, we're one to two years behind where we could have been if we'd always followed this principle. But our technology now helps us hear and see our customers' needs more clearly than ever before.

On a more personal note, even though my mom was the one whose experience as a real estate agent inspired me to start Compass in the first place, it took me a long time to solicit her advice and ideas — and take her feedback as seriously as it and she deserved. But now that I've come around, I've realized that she gives some of the most insightful feedback I get from anyone.

To do great things, do *many* things — and don't worry about the things that fail
The lesson I learned by launching something our customers hated

When you look up at the scoreboard, there's no number for misses. Points matter, not misses. If you score on your tenth try, you get the points no matter what happened before. (This is the extent of my sports knowledge. Sorry. Remember, I ran cross-country in high school.)

The same is true in business. If you come up with a single idea that changes the lives of your customers, that's all that matters. There are no points deducted for coming up with a lot of ideas that fail.

In fact, trying a lot of things that go nowhere is the best way to get somewhere amazing.

Everyone knows this. But so many people are still scared. They're terrified that if they try and fail they'll be seen as failures. The truth is, if you try and fail, you should be seen only as some-one who tries — and there's no higher honor than that.

A couple of years ago, we launched a program called Powered by Compass to license our software to other real estate broker-ages. It was a totally reasonable thing to try — a way to leverage our investment in software by selling it to others. But our agents hated this move. They were outraged. They felt that giving our technology to other brokerages that overlapped with their mar-ket undercut one of the core reasons why they joined Compass in the first place. So we listened, learned from reality, and canceled the program.

In my end-of-year email that year to the entire company, I mentioned Powered by Compass as one example in a long list of difficult things that we'd learned from in the past twelve months. When my internal email leaked to the media, some folks at Compass were worried that it made us look like we didn't know what we were doing.

Who launches and cancels a new project in the same month? they thought.

The answer is *Every successful entrepreneur does.*

It is infinitely better to try lots of things even if most fail than it is to spend your time in conference rooms worrying about the reasons that things *might not work.* Doing one great thing out of one hundred attempts is infinitely better than doing zero great things out of zero attempts.

The same year we launched Powered by Compass, we also launched a program called Compass Concierge, where we pay up-front for home-improvement services for any seller who wants to repaint, remodel, declutter, clean, or stage their home before putting it on the market. No fees, no interest.

Concierge has become the most important program we have ever launched in the history of Compass. But there is absolutely no way we would have created the wildly successful Compass Concierge without also trying the much-loathed Powered by Compass. They sprang from the same curious, experimental, entrepreneurial mentality. Both ideas had passionate champions as well as skeptical detractors. And in both cases, we chose to act and learn from reality rather than debate and avoid embarrassment.

I've come to believe that if you want to realize your potential it's better to focus on learning from failures than trying to *eliminate* failures.

4

BE SOLUTIONS DRIVEN

When everything seems to be going against you, remember that the airplane takes off against the wind, not with it.

— Henry Ford

Nothing is impossible. The word itself says "I'm possible!"

— Audrey Hepburn

Negativity is basically laziness. It takes a lot of hard work to remain positive, but positivity always pays off.

— RuPaul

Most people run from problems. Run toward them instead.

See every challenge, obstacle, and setback as an opportunity. Because in a world without problems, dreamers and innovators and entrepreneurs would have nothing to do. No reason for being. No chance to make a difference.

Make the impossible possible. Strive for solutions. Be a clear-eyed optimist who doesn't expect the path to be easy but believes that every obstacle can be overcome.

The difference between someone who gets stuck on a problem and someone who finds a solution isn't how smart they are or how many resources they have — it's how much energy and passion they can muster.

Surround yourself with people who give you energy and avoid anyone or anything who saps it. Seek out collaborators who share your mindset of abundance and possibility, the type of people who don't sit around thinking about how something might fail but get to work making sure that it succeeds.

When faced with a daunting challenge, say, "What if?" or "Here's a way we might be able to do it!" or "I don't like that idea, but here are three alternatives!" rather than giving up and simply saying, "No."

Remember that "no" is the killer of dreams, the killer of ideas, the end of a conversation. "No" halts momentum, interrupts flow, destroys energy. "No" leads nowhere. If you are going to say "no," it's your obligation to share alternative ideas to move the conversation forward to a solution.

Because unless someone can prove something is impossible, it's possible. All you need to do is find the solution.

Assume it's doable and then figure out how to get it done

The story of the hideous scaffolding on our flagship building

A little while back, our New York City headquarters underwent some facade maintenance. The crews put up ugly scaffolding that covered our address and the Compass sign, and made our entire building look like a construction site. Remember: real estate is about location and exposure, and suddenly our most prominent building was practically invisible. What's worse, it was scheduled to remain like that for about a year.

I was really unhappy that seemingly overnight an important asset that had made the company look great had become a liability that frustrated our agents and made us look bad.

I asked someone on the team to find a way to make it better. Maybe they could find a way to expedite the work? Or replace the scaffolding with something prettier? Or . . . something else? I didn't know the right answer and didn't have the time to solve it myself that week, but I knew I wanted something to change. And even though it seemed like a long shot, I truly believe that *anything* is possible.

After a number of weeks of looking into it, the team came back with bad news. The city had said that due to a variety of local ordinances there was nothing to be done. The contractor didn't have the time (or the inclination) to upgrade the scaffolding. And the work schedule was not up for discussion.

This was not good news. But I had a sense that something could still be done.

So I decided to ask someone else in the company, Rory Golod, the president of Compass Tri-State, if he could help.

Within seventy-two hours, I got a text and a picture from an agent on a Sunday. "The building looks phenomenal! It feels like we're BACK!" The scuffed-up off-green scaffolding that had been blocking our building was now draped with the largest, most beautiful banner I'd ever seen, emblazoned with the Compass name and logo many feet tall. It was *glorious*.

I called Rory and he picked up on the first ring. "How'd you do it?" I asked.

"Simple," he said. "I found some fine print in the law that says you're able to add your own branding if external construction is having an adverse effect on your business. I documented that that was happening, had the design team whip up a huge banner, got the sign company to work on the weekend, and I met them there earlier today to help install it."

Rory had been my chief of staff for several years earlier in his career. He knew how I approached problems better than almost anyone else in the company. He had heard what I said when people treated projects as if they were impossible.

"For ten minutes, let's pretend you had to do it. After ten minutes, you can say, 'It's impossible and I can't!' but for these ten minutes, tell me how you'd make it happen if you absolutely had to."

And "If this one problem or task were your *entire job,* how would you approach it?"

Rory had internalized those lessons. They'd become second nature to him. So he found a way. And in the process, he didn't just solve a problem, he created a spectacular solution. Buying a billboard on Fifth Avenue in New York City would have been ridiculously expensive, but our huge banner flew in front of our building for more than a year and a half — for free. When you walked through that part of town, you couldn't miss it.

Breakthrough ideas appear — seemingly out of nowhere — the second you stop blocking them with negativity, doubt, and day-to-day concerns like time, resources, and other responsibilities. That's the key.

Forcing your brain to believe something *is* possible often enables you to find the path that *makes* it possible; seeing how something *might* work in a perfect world helps you figure out how to *make* it happen in the real world. And before you know it, that big daunting project goes from impossible to *done.*

SIXTEEN THINGS MORE "IMPOSSIBLE" THAN WHATEVER CHALLENGE YOU'RE FACING

I believe that unless you can prove something is impossible it's possible.

So whenever you're feeling like the challenge you're facing is insurmountable, think through these fantastical-sounding accomplishments that have nonetheless already been achieved.

1. Discovering electricity — then bringing it to every home in America in the twentieth century
2. Ending slavery in America
3. Engineering a flying vehicle that weighs hundreds of tons and can soar through the air at hundreds of miles an hour while carrying hundreds of people
4. Measuring the size of the universe using only math and telescopes
5. Eradicating diseases that had killed hundreds of millions of people worldwide
6. Climbing Mount Everest and skiing to both the South Pole and the North Pole in a single lifetime
7. Walking on the moon and returning to Earth
8. Taking a heart from one person and putting it into the body of another person to save a life
9. Discovering DNA, sequencing it, then figuring out how to modify it letter by letter
10. Creating a supercomputer that fits in your pocket
11. Turning an online bookstore into a trillion-dollar company
12. Searching all of the world's information in less than a second
13. Building a map of the entire world that knows where you are and how to get anywhere you want to go

14. Creating "meat" without animals
15. Lifting a billion people out of abject poverty in the last twenty-five years
16. Battling a global pandemic

Look back at your to-do list now. Do you see anything that still looks *impossible*?

Spend your time with people who give you energy
Why I love young people who are the first in their family to go to college

There's no way I'd be where I am today if it hadn't been for the mentorship, professional development, summer internships, and support I received in high school and college. In the years since, I often found myself thinking about how many more young kids like me were out there struggling and how much more they could accomplish if they had just a bit of the good luck and support I had.

In 2009 I decided to start a nonprofit to help students from underprivileged backgrounds. I knew that two of the big challenges for me, then just twenty-nine years old, would be raising money and attracting mentors. To solve these problems, I thought that it was important to find a target student profile for the organization that would be the most inspirational for donors and mentors. There are many important causes to support, so I had to make sure that I could talk about helping students realize their college and career potential in a way that would be different and inspiring enough to attract meaningful support.

It wasn't easy.

I had just started dating Benís, who had this incandescent

energy that drew me to her from the first moment I met her. She was twenty-three and excited about her future; and the more I learned about her story, the more impressed I became. She told me with pride one day that she was the first person in her family to go to college.

It clicked. Who is more inspiring than students who are the first in their families to go to college, especially those coming from humble backgrounds? From my own life experience, I knew how hard it was to navigate college as an outsider, and as I learned more about Benís's story, I understood the sort of support these students needed even more clearly.

I knew that this was a problem that would inspire donors and mentors.

New York Needs You was born with the mission of helping kids who were the first in their families to go to college and who were living below the poverty line. (When we launched, that meant less than $29,500 for a family of four in New York City, a shockingly tiny amount to survive on.) We provided those students with the same types of support that had helped me so much in my own life: mentorship, professional development, summer internships, and college support.

Our research showed us that we'd be serving a real need: at the time, only 11 percent of students who were the first in their families to go to a four-year college and pursue a bachelor's degree ended up graduating. *Eleven percent!* And we knew we could marshal the right resources to help.

But the most important factor in our success was the students themselves. Their life stories were inspiring. Their passion was infectious. And the progress they made while working with us was tangible, visible, and transformational.

That wasn't just gratifying, it was essential to our success.

How else could we have convinced mentors to commit to donating two hundred hours of their time? Everyone involved was already working long hours at their day jobs. (This was the point in my life where I was going to the office seven days a week and running a marathon every month in a different state.) How else could we have hired terrific leaders to leave private-sector jobs to work longer hours for lower salaries?

The answer was always the students.

Students like Britanny Arboleda, who dropped out of high school but found a way to get back on track with a GED and entry into Bronx Community College. She was determined to persist—and she did. Britanny made history as the first student from BCC to transfer to Stanford, and she went there for free.

Students like Sheryll Pang Yu, who became a single mother at age nineteen and enrolled in community college just two months later to give her son a better future. After transferring to Baruch College, graduating, and working at the asset-management firm BlackRock, Sheryll launched her own start-up to empower parents with tools to engage their children in educational activities.

Every other weekend on a Saturday, we'd have these six-hour-long professional development programs in a meeting space donated by a company that one of us was connected to on Wall Street.

The location itself made a difference. Multiple students told us that they could see these buildings from where they lived, across the river, but had never dreamed they'd be inside of them, wearing business-casual clothing and talking about their careers.

We'd be in a room of one hundred students and one hundred mentors who were working intensively hour after hour. Elevator-pitch practice, project-management tutorials, mock interviews, résumé workshops. Videos, speakers, interactive breakout sessions, group work.

At the end of each daylong workshop, we'd do something we called Public and Private Victories. Anyone in the room could speak up and share something either about themselves or someone else. "I just got accepted into a four-year college!" or "I just got an internship for the summer" or "My mentor just got engaged." After each one, the room would erupt in cheering. Imagine hundreds of remarkable young students and hundreds of big-hearted mentors cheering for one another.

But I felt that same electric energy in our board meetings, which frequently ran until 1 or 2 a.m. We'd start each meeting by inviting a student in the program to share their experience with us and ask them each the same question, "What can we do better?"

We were all spending our days working in finance, law, consulting, banking, accounting, or private equity, and putting in long hours and tackling intellectually challenging problems, but we were not necessarily deriving deep satisfaction from our work.

But this—the chance to help young people change the trajectory of their lives—*this felt different*. As the nights wore on and we debated about the best ways to increase our impact, I felt immense gratitude for all of the people around the table—who didn't have to be there and probably would go home to finish up their normal work after our board meeting ended but didn't want to leave any more than I did.

Those people, who used every means at their disposal to show up for the brilliant and dedicated students we served, gave me so much energy. The students themselves gave me so much energy. Through their grit and passion, everyone involved powered everyone else to keep going. We were all there for one another because we knew we *had* to be there for the college students.

Since those early days, New York Needs You has become America Needs You. It has grown and scaled to serve students in multiple states and communities, and it's still going strong for the same reason it always has: because it's an endeavor that generates energy, passion, and progress for everyone who gets involved in any way.

There are two kinds of people in this world: people who give you energy and people who take it away. When I've collaborated with colleagues who don't inspire me or challenge me or give me a reason to be my best, work has felt like an endless slog. But when I've surrounded myself with people who do give me energy, it feels like there's always enough time in the day.

Find things that motivate you and hold them tightly
The four pictures I carried during my final marathon

I ran most of my first forty-nine marathons in around four hours. In truth, I was always happy to just cross the finish line. For my final marathon in my adopted hometown of New York City, however, I wanted to try something even bigger: to finish in less than three hours. That meant bringing my average nine-minute mile down to six and a half minutes or faster *for 26.2 miles in a row.*

I knew it wasn't going to be easy. So I trained for eight solid months at two different times, since the aftermath of Hurricane Sandy led to the cancellation of the 2012 marathon and I had to wait another full year and redo my eight long months of training to get ready for my fiftieth and final marathon.

A week out from the 2013 New York City Marathon, I was back in running shape — but I wasn't sure if I was going to be able to hit my goal time.

When you're running a marathon, the worst thing you can do is start too fast and run out of energy early. So you work on two things during training: finding a steady pace that you can hold for almost the entire race and learning to save up some of your energy so you can surge for your final twenty-eight minutes.

I knew that if I was going to break the three-hour barrier I would have to run the fastest final push I'd ever run and I knew that I'd need some sort of extra motivation to make that possible.

So I had the idea to bring four pictures with me that I knew would motivate me for different reasons. Each one would give me an extra boost during those last twenty-eight minutes — one picture for every seven minutes.

I made a plan to pull the photos out one by one during the race based on what each one meant to me and how motivational I thought it would be, saving the most energizing for last. I chose photos that brought out my strongest emotions: joy, love, hope, anger, yearning, determination.

I started with a picture of Benís and me on one of our first dates. It inspired a feeling of positivity in me as I thought about the future we'd build together and knowing that I had a friend who was really there for me.

The next one was a picture of me, my mom, my dad, and my half-brother Ricky taken when I was young. It made me sad because I could see that all that little boy wanted was to be around family — and that his family was broken apart. It made me mad that my mom never had the love and stability in her life that she was looking for.

With fourteen minutes left in the race, I took out the third picture, which gave me an incredibly high level of motivation. It was me as a toddler being held by my dad. I looked happy and I looked like I felt safe and taken care of by my father. I started crying with anger as I thought, *Why couldn't this little boy, this young me, get the love he so wanted from his father?* I started to think that every bad thought I have ever had was derived from this moment, the moment in my life when my dad left this little boy who deserved love—and it made me run fast and hard with pain and a yearning to be with my father and tell him that I loved him even though he had left and even though he was dead. That I loved him regardless. And I ran even faster.

And then I transitioned to my last source of motivation: my baby girl, Raia. I told myself in those final seven and a half minutes that I would never let that little girl feel the way I had felt. That I would protect her and love her and give her the security and fatherhood I never had. And that gave me the drive to unleash every last ounce of energy in my body. To run for the future. To run for the family I was creating.

I crossed the finish line of my final marathon in two hours, fifty-nine minutes, and thirty-one seconds. After running more than twenty-six miles, I'd beaten my goal by twenty-nine seconds. I crossed the finish line, fell on my knees, and broke down in tears.

Over the years, I've realized that the lesson I learned that day about how to motivate myself—how to transform loss, anger, and negativity into *positive* energy—was actually a much bigger accomplishment than finishing a marathon in record time. By paying attention to my own emotions and noticing the impact they have on my energy levels, I've learned when and how to call up a memory of someone who doubted me or abandoned me or hurt me—and that's helped inspire me to do everything I've done since.

The first question to ask if you want a raise
My friend and the advice he had trouble hearing

A friend recently asked me about how he should negotiate for a better compensation package at his job. (This was someone who does not work at Compass.)

I asked him to tell me a little about the situation so I could provide more useful advice.

He told me that he needed to make more money due to his family situation. He told me how long it had been since he'd gotten a raise. He told me how important it was to him for his hard work to be recognized.

What he didn't tell me was anything about his manager or his company's goals.

We're old friends, so I knew him well enough to be blunt. "It doesn't matter what *you* want, it matters what *they* want."

Obviously, what he wanted matters — to him. But to get someone to do something for you, you need to first think about them.

But he kept returning to all of his reasons why he felt he should get a raise and why it was only fair for him to get one.

So I tried to make my recommendation even clearer. Whenever you're building your case for a raise or a promotion, you should always start with a simple question: Who in the organization can't accomplish their goals or achieve their dreams without you?

If the answer is nobody, then it's going to be difficult to get a raise. But assuming there is someone who can't accomplish their goals or achieve their dreams without you, talk to that person first. That's because this person has the most incentive for you to be happy and productive, and will be the most motivated to help you achieve your goal. Ask this person how best to ground your request in the results you're going to drive. Once you've learned how to show that you're indispensable, it's much easier to be treated like you are.

It finally clicked for my friend.

And his raise followed shortly after.

5

OBSESS ABOUT OPPORTUNITY

To succeed, work hard, never give up and above all cherish a magnificent obsession.

— Walt Disney

No one changes the world who isn't obsessed.

— Billie Jean King

Don't start a company unless it's an obsession and something you love. If you have an exit strategy, it's not an obsession.

— Mark Cuban

You should obsess about every opportunity to improve your customers' lives.

Small things. Big things. Easy things. Hard things. Audacious efforts that will blow customers away. Tiny details that will make the experience a little bit more delightful.

Obsessing about opportunity creates *opportunities; the closer you look, the more you'll see. If something might matter to the customer, it should be a matter of great importance to you.*

Be obsessive. *Care more than it makes any sense to care. In a world where many people think "okay" is okay and "good enough" is good enough,* actually caring *is a huge competitive advantage.*

Every successful entrepreneur is obsessed about the opportunity in front of them. Try to imagine Jeff Bezos saying that Amazon's delivery speed had gotten "fast enough." Or Beyoncé only going through the motions on stage. Or Reed Hastings at Netflix saying that they already had a lot of great shows and didn't need to try to make another breakout hit. It would never happen.

Problems are opportunities. Look for things that are not as beautiful as they could be. Or more expensive than they ought to be. Tasks that are inefficient or too complicated. See the opportunities everywhere around you to get better.

If you want to just have a job and a paycheck, well, get a job with a paycheck. But if you want to do something meaningful with your life, find a passion and an opportunity that you can't stop obsessing about. And never look back.

Relationships are always a good investment

Compass wouldn't exist if I hadn't sent holiday cards to a guy I met once at a dinner

When I was a White House Fellow, I was invited to an American Academy of Achievement conference honoring world leaders and new inductees. During one of the dinners, I was seated next to a very interesting individual. We were both young, ambitious guys in our midtwenties, and we quickly bonded over our mutual connections to Israel, where both he and my mother were born.

But there was one big difference between the two of us: Ori had just sold his first company to Google earlier that year. It was a search algorithm called Orion that he'd developed as a PhD computer science project. Now that he was a Google employee, he was integrating his code into their main Google Search algorithm.

We had a fascinating conversation over surprisingly good food, but the relationship could easily have ended after dessert.

However, my mother always taught me to invest in relationships even if you had no idea where they might lead. So I gave Ori my card, got his information, and sent him a handwritten note a few days later to thank him for the conversation, and I pledged to stay in touch.

Normally, "let's stay in touch" is a phrase that people *say* — not something that people actually *do*. But when the holidays rolled around that year, I mailed Ori another handwritten card and told him that we should get together again next time we are in the same city. He took me up on it.

Over the next six years, I kept sending him holiday cards and birthday cards, and catching up occasionally. During that time, he left Google, started a second tech company called Julpan, asked me to be an advisor, and proceeded to sell that start-up to Twitter a year after founding it.

Needless to say, I was very impressed. Everyone I knew dreamed of launching a successful start-up — and Ori had already done it *twice* by his early thirties.

So when I started to dream about starting my own company and was looking for a cofounder, Ori was my first call. Over the years, he'd certainly proven his prowess in the world of tech start-ups, and he told me that my persistent and thoughtful communication convinced him I was the kind of person who did what I said I would do. Someone he could trust.

It wasn't especially *fun* to write and send cards every year to thousands of people during every holiday season. It was a lot of work. Hours and hours and hours of sitting alone in the evenings writing out addresses and dipping my stamp in hot wax to seal each envelope.

And most of these relationships had no tangible benefit to me over the years. But they all gave me a sense of community and connection across the city I loved and the wider world that I wanted to explore. They've made me feel like I'm never truly alone even when I'm working alone.

And many of the relationships were even more rewarding than that. There is Ori, of course, but also hundreds of other people I've worked with or collaborated with over the years. I've spent more time investing in my relationships than any other person I've ever met. And I have never regretted a single minute of it.

Bias isn't just wrong — it blinds you to opportunity

How negative stereotypes about real estate agents
created opportunity for Compass

Diversity is good. Discrimination is bad. Inclusion is good. Bias is bad.

We all know that these things are true, but too many people think of them as values that are nice to embrace when possible but not truly mission critical for their business.

The reality is that bias and discrimination don't just hurt the people who are targeted — they also hurt the people who are acting discriminatorily.

Every employer who has passed over a brilliant potential employee of color because of some irrelevant "culture fit" issue is missing out on the extraordinary contributions that person could have brought. Every company that fails to promote a woman to a management position because she doesn't fit their notion of what "leadership looks like" is being led more poorly because of their shortsightedness.

On a different level, Compass had more time and space to grow because so many people have internalized our society's inaccurate stereotype of real estate agents — leaving a gargantuan business opportunity largely overlooked and a millions-strong group of small-business owners terribly underserved.

Because agents are often stereotyped in negative ways, well-financed start-ups have naively focused on eliminating real estate agents instead of empowering them.

Compass has been able to grow largely unchallenged by other start-ups because other businesses in the space have let their assumptions about real estate agents drive their strategy. They *assume* that real estate agents don't provide any real value, so they try to build technology to replace them. They *assume* real estate agents are overcharging clients, so they try to invent models without commissions.

I know how deeply this bias runs because I've felt it *myself* — even though my own mother, who I love and respect, is an agent. When we launched Urban Compass in 2012, we thought we could create a better model for renters than relying on real estate agents. But within a year, I realized that agents weren't overvalued — they were *undervalued*. I saw how hard they worked, how selfless they were, how deeply they cared for their clients, and how difficult it was for us to replicate even a tenth of their skills with technology. They deserved to be elevated, not eliminated.

The Compass team decided that the best role we could play in the world was to be the champion of the one of the largest groups of entrepreneurs in America: real estate agents. Not because it was cool or popular but because it was a massive business opportunity that others were blind to — and because we cared about the entrepreneurs we were able to help.

The financial argument was extraordinarily clear: there are two million agents in the United States alone who bring in roughly $90 billion annually in commissions. If we could help agents become more successful, we would be successful. If we could create economic value for agents, then that would create equity value for Compass. While others scoffed at agents and tried to disrupt them, we set to work helping them save time, eliminate hassle, serve clients more seamlessly, and grow their businesses. And we haven't looked back since.

FOUR REASONS TO BE GRATEFUL

As much as possible, I like to focus on the positives in my life rather than dwell on the difficulties. It's one of the ways I generate and sustain the energy I need to do everything I want to do every day and every week and every year. If you're struggling to see the bright side, here are four things to appreciate that I guarantee will be true for any person who is reading this book.

Be grateful for:

1. The ways that the struggles and challenges you've faced have shaped you into the person you are and have made you stronger
2. Every bit of luck, circumstance, and privilege that you've benefited from in your life that have enabled you to have the time to learn, read, and grow
3. Living now rather than at any other time when violence,

poverty, disease, and injustice were even worse than they are today and when so many marvels of science and progress, however unequally distributed, didn't even exist yet

4. The miraculous, improbable, impossible blessing that is human existence — the result of billions of years of evolution

And don't stop there. Gratefulness is like love: the more you give, the more you get. The more gratitude you feel in a day, the more you'll have to be grateful for.

Always look for the positive even when it's hard to see
The lessons I learned leading during the coronavirus pandemic

When the coronavirus pandemic first hit, I was going to work every day in Compass's eleven-story office building in Manhattan, riding elevators, meeting with hundreds of people a week, flying to Seattle twice a month to meet with the leaders of our West Coast technology hub, and visiting other Compass offices in other cities.

Then, in a matter of days, everything changed. First came the official declaration that the coronavirus was a pandemic. Then the stock market crashed, evaporating trillions of dollars in wealth and savings. Then came the urgent shelter-in-place orders.

Like the rest of the country, we closed all of our offices and everyone began to work from home. My extended family and I locked down together: Benís; our three children; both of our mothers; my best friend, Jabali; and his son. I instantly went from being constantly on the move to being constantly in one place. I stopped shaking hundreds of hands per week and started shaking the hand of just one person: my one-year-old son, River, who would wrap his entire little hand around one of my fingers as he tried to learn to walk.

Between employees and agents, Compass was nearly 20,000 people strong at that point. An energetic, outgoing community of collaborators who suddenly found themselves physically isolated from one another, worried about their health and safety, and very unsure about their businesses and their future.

There I was, sitting at my laptop in a hastily converted office with bare shelves behind me trying to figure out how to set up better lighting and sound for the back-to-back video meetings that made up my entire workday while hearing my family trying to figure out remote schooling in the next room.

Ken Chenault had taught me that in order to be a leader for others you have to be able to do three things: be able to ground yourself in reality, articulate a vision of where you want to go, and outline a clear path to get there. But in the midst of unprecedented uncertainty — when the on-the-ground reality was changing so much every day — I realized that leadership was as much about daily communication and mindset as it was about having a strategic plan.

During those early months of the pandemic, I doubled down on the abundance mindset that has guided me throughout my life (even before I knew the term). It's the idea that "there will always be more" rather than the scarcity mindset of "there will never be enough." It's the difference between believing that the pie is getting bigger and believing that the pie is shrinking, between thinking big and embracing risk and thinking small and avoiding risk, between embracing change or fearing change.

It might seem like having a positive mindset during historically challenging times is impossible — or at least insufficient. But I found the opposite. When there's so much you cannot control in the world around you, changing your mindset is one of the easiest and most powerful things you can do. It's something that you can completely control yourself.

Rather than saying, "I hate being stuck inside," I chose to say, "I'm happy that I'm healthy and have a safe place to be with my family."

Rather than focusing on all the ways our business was hurt by the (very wise and necessary) stay-at-home orders, I encouraged the team to look for unexpected opportunities. Our company's strategy is to empower real estate agents to grow and thrive — how could we keep doing that in this new environment?

It turned out that the thousands of Compass entrepreneurs who were stuck at home and unable to work with clients now had more time than ever to grow professionally. We revamped Compass Academy, our internal online learning platform, and opened it up to the public.

It turned out that many home buyers and sellers still wanted — or needed — to move, so our software engineers built tools to help agents host virtual open houses and virtual tours safely and securely. In fact, we launched almost twice as much new technology during the first six months of the pandemic than we had in the six months prior.

Even with a positive attitude, those early weeks and months were not easy for any of us.

But with the health and safety of our community as our number one priority and in the face of uncertainty, stress, sadness, and confusion, we have chosen to embrace a hopeful and bountiful mindset. None of us are coming out of this crisis unchanged. But whatever the new normal ends up being, we will remain obsessed about the opportunity to serve our customers, embrace change, and create an ever more abundant world.

6

COLLABORATE WITHOUT EGO

You can design and create, and build the most wonderful
place in the world. But it takes people to make the dream
a reality.

— Walt Disney

There are two kinds of people, those who do the work and
those who take the credit. Try to be in the first group; there
is less competition there.

— Indira Gandhi

The strength of the team is each individual member. The
strength of each member is the team.

— Phil Jackson

*All businesses — all human endeavors, in fact — are powered by
people and sustained through relationships.*

Ask yourself what sort of people you like to work with — then strive to be like that every single day. Be reliable and responsive, collaborative and curious. Ask for blunt feedback and listen carefully when it's delivered — learning from reality is far more important than protecting your ego.

To thrive in business — and in life — you'll need customers, colleagues, employees, partners, and mentors. Treat every relationship with respect and care. Inspire everyone you interact with during the day to feel like they want to work with you again tomorrow. Give credit and thanks freely knowing you'll be repaid handsomely in other ways.

Go through the world with the knowledge that it takes a long time to build trust but only a single moment to destroy it.

Check your ego because high-functioning teams deliver the best results — and outsize egos make teamwork nearly impossible. If you try to get ahead by trampling others, you may succeed today but only by destroying the promise of tomorrow.

Collaborate without ego because your dreams are too big to realize on your own — and too important to give up on. Collaborate without ego because no one succeeds alone.

Values aren't what you say, they're who you fire
The first time we fired a high-producing agent

It's easy to think that your values are defined by your mission statement or some pretty words listed on your website. But articulating your principles isn't nearly enough.

Culture is defined by what you *do.* Your values are revealed in how you treat people in the moments when no one's watching. Your principles shine when you follow them even when it goes against some incentive or interest. Doing what's right when it's hard — *that* is how you live your values.

I remember the week I learned this. It was a very stressful and confusing time, and I wasn't sure if I was making the right call. It was only when I saw how people reacted afterward that I knew my gut had led me to the correct decision.

In the early years of Compass, there was a very successful agent who was making us a lot of money. But we had heard from a young woman who worked for this superstar agent that he had been quite cruel to her. And it wasn't an isolated incident — apparently, there was a pattern of yelling and belittling that made her feel disrespected and unsafe. It was the sort of behavior that our values told us we should have absolutely zero tolerance for.

At the same time, it wasn't easy. If we fired him, would other high-performing agents leave with him? Would people in the industry who knew his reputation for success think that something was wrong with Compass instead of him? With so much potentially lost revenue on the line, was his behavior really *that* bad? Those doubts led me to drag my feet for much longer than I should have.

In the end, we decided that living our values was more important than anything else. That even if it stalled our growth or spooked other agents, it was worth it to us to do the right thing. So we made the call and immediately showed the agent the door.

That was on a Friday, and by Monday, the news had spread throughout the entire company. It's not like we did anything heroic, we just did what felt right without letting our worries about the consequences cloud our vision.

But people said, "Wow, you really are a different kind of company." They told me their old brokerages would have looked the other way for an agent who was that successful. Like I almost did.

Firing that agent didn't only help strengthen our culture — it also helped strengthen our business. Standing by our values even when they went against our financial interests in the moment attracted many more top agents to Compass who collectively brought in far more revenue than that one top producer ever would have on his own. But even if that hadn't turned out to be true, I would still have felt that it was the right call.

And I think you'd be surprised how many times listening to your conscience actually helps your business. There's a common myth that you have to be ruthless in order to get ahead, but I've found the opposite to be true. Nice people succeed much more often than mean people. And they sleep better at night, too.

To recruit, align your needs with their story
How we hired the number one agent in New York City when Compass was just one year old

In the early years of Compass, we made a big pivot from hiring quickly trained neighborhood specialists who helped people rent apartments to recruiting highly experienced real estate agents who helped people buy and sell homes.

That meant we had to attract a lot of experienced agents. But agents were skeptical of us. We were still very new. We knew more about technology and business than we did about the real estate industry.

To shift that perception and build trust, we needed to hire a top real estate agent who had earned enough admiration from their peers to instantly make others take us seriously.

As always, my first step was to learn from reality, so I asked ten New York City agents I was trying to recruit to give me three names of agents they respected deeply and would want to work with. There was only one name that showed up on all ten lists: Leonard Steinberg.

Leonard was a legend and he was at the top of his game. He was the number one agent in New York. In the previous year, he'd sold or contracted for more than $500 million in real estate.

We knew why we needed him, but we had no idea why he might need us.

So we started to get to know him by inviting him to a roundtable discussion we were holding with top agents in the city to help us learn about all the ways they wanted the industry to change.

We became experts in all things Leonard Steinberg. Born in Cape Town, South Africa, he started out his career as a fashion designer for Victor Costa and Christian Dior America, launched his own fashion label, tried his hand as a pianist and composer, then found his place in the real estate business at age thirty-one.

We weren't the only company pursuing him. Leonard had talked to or met with people from every major brokerage in New York in the months before coming to Compass.

Ori and I knew that to convince someone great to join your company you need to focus less on what *you* need and more on how you can contribute to *their* story. How would taking this job advance the plot of Leonard's life? Which of his problems does it solve? What future does it help unlock for him?

Over the course of multiple months, we had countless meals, discussions, calls, and meetings with Leonard, and his story slowly came into focus.

The fact that he led the number one agent team in New York City meant to him that he had nowhere else to go. He thrived off challenges and was looking for his next one.

He was a maverick who liked seeing opportunity where others didn't. He liked proving people wrong, and like me, he got energy from people who doubted him or his ideas. The fact that

Compass was so untested and underestimated turned out to be a major selling point for Leonard.

He was extremely thoughtful and opinionated about everything, but despite being universally respected in the industry, he didn't have a way to turn his ideas into actual impact. He saw dignity and nobility in the role of the agent, and he wanted to help elevate and modernize the reputation of the profession. He wanted to shape the future of the industry he'd grown to love.

He'd already made more money than he had ever dreamed of, but in real estate, even if you sell a $25 million penthouse, you wake up the next morning stressed about what you'll do next. Leonard was looking to be part of building something more permanent and substantial.

Many people had suggested that Leonard should start his own company, but the idea of operating a business himself sounded like a chore. He wanted to be able to help lead a company without having to *run* it.

He was also frustrated with the current state of technology in real estate — it was like a "bake sale from the '80s," he once said — and the fact that new tech tools were being built without consulting agents and with the clear goal of eliminating them in the long run drove him crazy. He wanted to have a seat at the table so he could help designers and software engineers build technology that actually empowered agents and made their lives better.

Learning all those things about Leonard took a lot of time and genuine curiosity, but they helped us shape a role around him and the future he saw for himself. Leonard's underlying motivation, we discovered, was to find a leadership position that would allow him to help transform our industry and create a better future for real estate agents.

Ori was the one who thought of using an analogy to Apple,

which had always had great tech talent but had only become wildly successful because they were guided by a well-respected visionary with strong opinions and the ability to advocate for their customers.

With this in mind, Ori told Leonard, "We have some of the best software engineers from places like Google and incredible business minds from places like McKinsey and Goldman, but we need our Steve Jobs. We need someone like you to build trust with the real estate world and make sure we're building technology that agents love."

In that moment, I saw in Leonard's eyes that he'd committed to joining Compass.

The week before Leonard started, Ori and I visited his beautiful home and he gave us the full tour. Above his desk — as hard as this is to believe — was a rare signed photograph of Steve Jobs. I remember looking at Ori after we both saw the photograph and smiling. Ori hadn't just been perceptive — he'd also been lucky. Even though Leonard would never compare himself to Steve Jobs, he was deeply inspired by the type of difference Jobs had made.

Still, Leonard's deciding to come to Compass was a big risk for him. (I cannot understate how unlikely it was that a one-year-old start-up was hiring the number one agent in the biggest city in America.) But it was a calculated risk that he had taken the time to get both his head and his heart behind.

As we expected, hiring Leonard Steinberg as president of Compass made major waves in the industry. A trade publication said it was the "shot heard 'round the real estate world."

But he didn't join to help us get that press; he joined because it was good for the arc of his life and the legacy he would leave behind. "The most important thing to me was that the future was exciting and interesting," he told the media. Responding to the doubt and disbelief of his colleagues, he said, "It's a dangerous thing to pass judgment too soon. I think we're going to surprise a lot of people." Eight years later, we've done just that — and we plan on doing it together for many more years to come.

We spent much more time recruiting Leonard than we do with most hires, but throughout *every* hiring process, it's important to think of *their* story more than *your* needs and highlight the harmony between the two. This approach has helped us to recruit fantastic people and propel them forward once they arrive. Ideally, on their first day, every new hire already knows that their journey and our journey are heading in the same direction — and that the more passion they pour into their work, the more progress they'll make toward their own goals.

FIVE TESTS FOR HIRING AND FIRING

I never did that well on tests in school, but there are a number of simple tests that I've found helpful in professional life. They're valuable because the more we think about something, the more our minds try to play tricks on us. We second-guess, we let doubt and fear creep in, we hesitate, we overthink. The purpose of these tests is to get past all that and get back to the truth that you've known deep down all along.

This is especially true regarding the two most important decisions you make as a manager: whether to hire someone and whether it's time to let someone go.

1. **The "good person" test.** If you have to pause when you ask yourself, *Is this a good person?* they shouldn't be on your team.

    Lots of people think goodness doesn't matter at work

— and some people even think it's a liability in business. Not me. If everyone we work with is a good person, we'll all be better off. Do they live by the Golden Rule? Is their heart in the right place? Are they kind? Do they genuinely care about others? Do they want to give back?

2. **The energy test.** Does this person give me energy or take it away?

Entrepreneurship is all about energy. You'll dream bigger and move faster if the people you're collaborating with give you energy rather than drain the energy out of you. When you're figuring out which people to collaborate with closely, find the ones who make you more excited to come into work each morning. They'll help you bring out your best self — and, odds are, you'll do the same for them.

3. **The "another offer" test.** Ask yourself, *If this person came to you tomorrow and told you they had a great offer from another company, would you fight to keep them?*

This one originated at Netflix, where they believe that excellent people are much better than "pretty good" people. This test helps you admit that someone isn't excellent. As the speaker Jim Rohn says, "You are the average of the five people you spend the most time with." If you want to be better — like I know all of us do — one of the best ways is to make sure you're surrounding yourself with exceptional people.

4. **The rationalization test.** If your key argument for someone or something is not related to actual results, you're probably trying to rationalize something you shouldn't be.

An example of this is when people say, "This person has been around for a long time and is really good for culture."

I believe that culture is incredibly important, but if the person was truly great, you'd say, "This person is great and has great impact. We clearly don't want to lose them."
5. **The principles test.** How well does a potential hire embody each of the eight entrepreneurship principles?

The idea of "culture fit" can be a code word for a lot of discrimination. If you ask people to prioritize "culture" without defining your culture, there's a risk that they will gravitate toward people like them. It's another trick our minds play on us.

At Compass, our culture is entrepreneurial, so whenever I'm hiring or doing reviews, I evaluate people on how well they dream big, move fast, learn from reality, are solutions driven, obsess about opportunity, collaborate without ego, maximize their strengths, and bounce back with passion.

Everyone's responsible = no one's responsible
If no one owns the problem, you have a problem

When I started Compass, I'd never been a CEO before. I was lucky that Ori had run two successful companies already, so he coached me through the first year or so. I listened carefully to him as we built out the organization and developed the ways of working together that got us off the ground and headed in the right direction.

But as anyone who's ever led a team knows, managing people is not a set-it-and-forget-it situation. To excel, you need to observe and experiment all the time to identify what's working and what's not, try out new solutions, and scale up the ones that make a difference. Over the first few years, I'd come to expect a need for some sort of significant change to the way we were working every six to twelve months.

Which is why, at one point in our fourth year, I wasn't surprised that another problem had arisen that needed solving.

It seemed that people were spending more time trying to figure out what to do and less time delivering results. The company had grown in complexity, everyone was increasingly specialized, and most projects required participation from different departments with different priorities. Our pace and our progress had slowed.

But it took me a little while to understand one of the biggest reasons why. And then it became clear during an otherwise unremarkable conversation with two colleagues from legal and finance.

We were negotiating a partnership with another company, and I asked for an update on the deal terms. I had already asked a few times over email but hadn't gotten a clear answer. I started to get the sense that there wasn't one person who owned the problem and had the answer. So when the three of us had the chance to get in a room together to talk, I asked directly: "What's going on?"

One of them said, "What we're doing is —"

"Who's 'we'?," I asked. "I don't understand who is doing what. Specifically."

As it turned out, both of them thought that the other person was going to answer. Throughout the project, they were deferring to each other. The project had fallen behind schedule because it had fallen through the space between them.

I realized a few things at once. It wasn't their fault; it was *my* fault for not yet creating a culture of accountability. It wasn't an isolated issue. And it was happening in hundreds of ways across the company.

So we came up with a new designated role that has unlocked a huge amount of potential and helped us avoid a huge amount of confusion, and we coined a new acronym, SPOA, which stands for Single Point of Accountability.

For every project that requires collaboration, we assign one person to be the SPOA. They're responsible for driving it forward, unsticking jams, clarifying confusion, and solving problems. They don't have to do the entire project, of course, but they do need to make sure it gets done and that everyone knows what they need to do to get it done. And when anyone needs an update on a project, the SPOA is the person who can answer.

Because, while no one succeeds alone, we all get a lot more done together when it's clear who's leading on what.

7

MAXIMIZE YOUR STRENGTHS

Everybody is a genius. But if you judge a fish by its ability to climb a tree, it will live its whole life believing that it is stupid.

— Often attributed to Albert Einstein

Happiness comes from being who you actually are instead of who you think you are supposed to be.

— Shonda Rhimes

Don't ask what the world needs. Ask yourself what makes you come alive, and go do that, because what the world needs is people who have come alive.

— Howard Thurman

We live in a society that's obsessed with people's weaknesses. Not strong enough. Not good enough. Not fast enough. Not smart enough.

Imagine a world where everyone was recognized every day for their strengths *instead? Imagine a world where everyone was able to be their best selves? Imagine a world where everyone did what they excelled at all the time?*

How satisfying would that be?

How energizing?

How empowering?

If you want to be your best self, you must be your authentic self. If you want to reach your full potential, you must maximize your strengths. But to maximize your strengths, you must first get to know yourself well enough to identify *your strengths and* accept *your weaknesses.*

That process is neither quick nor easy, but it can be transformational. *Your imperfections are what make you perfect. The very things that make you stand out also make you outstanding. Understanding these truths unlocks your ability to perform at a level you've never dreamed of before.*

Don't waste time beating yourself up. Lean into the things you love. Don't try to be someone you're not. Pour your passion into getting even better at the things you're great at. Don't fixate on your weaknesses. Surround yourself with people whose strengths complement your own. And don't stop searching until you've found a place where you can be yourself and truly belong.

So many people go to bed at night thinking about their failures, what they didn't do right that day. I ask you to go to bed at night thinking about your strengths *and your* dreams. *And wake up each morning ready to be your best, truest, and most powerful self.*

Be grateful for your struggles; they made you who you are

Disowned, abandoned, and . . . lucky?

It seems almost mathematically obvious to say that your life would be better if it didn't include the bad parts.

But it's not true.

The truth is, your life experiences don't just happen to you, they actually make you who you are. If you remove all of the hardship, adversity, and struggle from your life, you would no longer be *you*. Human beings are shockingly complex organisms; you can't change one thing about yourself without affecting every other part.

I've suffered a lot because my dad left us and my grandparents disowned us. But if I hadn't felt that pain, I wouldn't be me. I'd be some other person instead.

Not fitting in anywhere, I've always had to adapt, and that hasn't always been easy, but the truth is, my adaptability has been crucial to every success I've ever achieved.

Not having a father figure to rely on, I've cultivated relationships with hundreds of mentors over my life. I was filling a void in my heart — but I was also building a network that has given me more life-changing advice and opened more doors than any one father ever could.

Not having family resources to fall back on, I've always felt an intense drive to accomplish enough as soon as possible so even if everything fell apart, I'd still have the financial security to support my family and my mom in her old age. I can be restless and relentless, but those traits have helped me move faster and help more people than I ever would have been able to otherwise.

If my life had been easy from day one, would I have become a complete screw-up instead?

If I somehow had the choice to choose between the life I had — with an abusive, heroin-addicted father and grandparents who chose not to meet me because of my race — and a "perfect" life with a loving father and caring grandparents, I honestly don't know what I'd choose.

But I don't have a choice. And neither do you. Our struggles are part of us. It's not that challenges in life are noble or beneficial, it's that they're universal and irreversible. We've all had hardships of one sort or another. The only choice we have is how much we learn from them and how we react to them.

The same is generally true for our family backgrounds. I cannot count the number of times I was asked the oddest question during high school, college, and early in my career, "What do your parents do?" For years, I felt ashamed that I didn't have a better answer. The best I could say about my dad was that he'd been a carpenter, but even that felt like I was leaving more out than I was telling.

But one day while I was at Goldman Sachs, I heard a partner say with pride that his father had been a fireman — and I realized I could have that same pride in my own past even if it didn't involve yachts or summer houses. Throughout the professional world, I saw that many of the most successful people came from relatively humble beginnings. At Goldman, I learned that Henry Cornell was born and raised in the Bronx by a single mother. Ray McGuire grew up in inner-city Dayton, Ohio, and was also raised by a single mother. The more people I got to know, the more stories like these I heard. It was empowering to realize that I could be my authentic self instead of having to hide myself.

I no longer merely accept my struggles and my background, I'm actually grateful for them. They gave me the motivation to succeed and the determination to have a positive impact on the world around me. As I've learned to accept and value myself, I've developed an appreciation for everything—good and bad—that made me exactly who I am.

Instead of fixating on your weaknesses, focus on your strengths

A better way to read a report card

Can you imagine an NFL coach telling a linebacker that throwing fifty-yard passes is one of his weaknesses and that he should work on that? Or a soccer coach telling Megan Rapinoe, America's superstar forward, that she ought to work on her goalkeeping skills?

Of course not. In sports, it's clear that you should focus on maximizing your strengths—and play with a team of people whose strengths complement your weaknesses.

The same is true in business. You don't rely on your accountant to lay out an inspiring ten-year vision or ask your head of sales to redesign your logo. Your team needs someone who's good with numbers, someone who's visionary, someone who can sell, and someone who knows branding. They clearly don't have to all be the same person.

As far as I can remember, my teachers always focused on the areas where I was struggling more than the areas where I was excelling. In high school, they would tell me to focus on bringing up a C grade rather than more deeply exploring my passions and interests, where I was earning As.

This obsession with report cards and GPAs made me feel like

I was always failing no matter how many subjects I was actually doing well in.

I'm not saying that you shouldn't push yourself to try new things when you are young—even if they're hard or don't come naturally to you—in order to discover your strengths and expand your horizons.

But once successful people are grown up and in the real world, they focus more on maximizing their strengths than obsessing about their weaknesses. I was a C student in high school and college, but I was also someone who was dreaming of things much bigger than a straight-A report card. Fixating on your weaknesses is debilitating. Focusing on your strengths is electrifying.

I've found that the more time I spend doing the things I'm truly passionate about and truly excellent at, the better my life becomes. Don't get me wrong, it's still important to acknowledge my weaknesses and mitigate their impact, but I try to put almost all of my energy—my most valuable resource—into leveraging my strengths.

Trying to be someone else isn't fun and doesn't work
"Look, you're never going to be a great analyst"
Starting out at McKinsey was really challenging.

I felt like I didn't belong, but maybe that was because it was a new place and I hadn't yet fallen into a good rhythm with the other analysts. I also felt like I wasn't very good at the work, but maybe that was because I was just learning a challenging set of skills.

As a result, I worked extremely long hours to try to get up to speed and become successful, but I couldn't shake the worry that I was always about to be fired. I had heard of impostor syndrome —the common feeling that you truly don't belong in your job and you're going to be revealed as a fraud at any moment — and I sometimes chalked up my stress to that.

But when I talked to the other first-year analysts, they appeared to be enjoying their experience a lot more than I was. There was one analyst in particular who just *loved* the work. I'll never forget his face. I didn't just want to be as good as he was (or better), I found myself actually wanting to *be* him.

But I wasn't. I couldn't be. And the harder I tried to be like him, the worse I felt about myself.

During my first performance review, my manager said, "Look, Robert, you're never going to be a great analyst," in a tone that many people would have taken very hard. But I took that comment as a gift. It felt both clarifying and freeing.

And when my manager followed up with "But you've got some real spikes" — the McKinsey term for strengths — "and you should focus on maximizing those," I started to see the path toward accepting myself for who I was and what I was good at.

He was right that I was never going to "spike" at poring over statistics and building financial models like that other analyst. If I put every ounce of effort into it, I could, perhaps, become good at those skills — but I'd never be *great*. That work would never make me come alive.

I'd been pushing myself to my limits for months and beating myself up whenever I fell short. That sort of "no pain, no gain" attitude seemed like the only way to live at the time. And don't get me wrong, painful work does yield amazing results sometimes. Training for a marathon, for example, isn't fun — but it works.

The painful work of trying to be someone else, however, is both unpleasant *and* ineffective.

And yet, so many of us do it every day. We see someone else — someone with a completely different life story, different circumstances, a different personality, different gifts — and we want to be them rather than ourselves. It leads nowhere. It accomplishes nothing. And it feels terrible.

On the other hand, seeing your own strengths as useful and important and accepting that your own weaknesses are never going to dramatically change leads somewhere productive. Understanding that the only person you can ever be is yourself — and that this is not just a reality but a blessing — can point you to the path your life ought to take.

That's not to say it's easy or quick, though. Even after I knew that I'd be more fulfilled and more successful if I maximized my strengths, it took me a long time to actually embrace that mindset in my life.

Six long years after I'd gotten that tough performance review at McKinsey, my manager at Goldman Sachs, Henry Cornell, sat me down and gave me a nearly identical talk. He said, "Robert, you are never going to be the best at Excel spreadsheets and financial analysis. Instead of trying to make your weakness a strength, focus on minimizing your weaknesses and maximizing your strengths. You have great strengths like relationship building, and you could be bringing in deals."

But I didn't act on my managers' advice until I started Compass, where I've built my role to allow me to spend as much time as possible doing what I'm best at and selected my team to be strong where I am not. I've learned that one of my strengths is connecting with our customers — the real estate agents we serve at Compass — so I spend an unusual amount of my time doing that and translating their ideas and needs into our product road map, marketing efforts, and more. And I recruited a truly exceptional chief financial officer to be the excellent analyst I never was and lead the financial strategy of the company. We all balance one another, support one another, and allow one another to be our best selves.

I just wish I hadn't waited so long.

Sometimes the best way to help your kids is to help yourself
Why my first manager didn't move to the suburbs

Early in my career, many of the executives at McKinsey lived with their families in the suburbs in large houses with outdoor space. But Dick Foster, a senior partner at the firm, chose to live with his family in Manhattan in an apartment.

When I asked him why, Dick said something that stuck with me: "New York City makes me happy and a happy father is a good father." He loved the city; the energetic pace, the diversity of opportunities, and the cosmopolitan lifestyle were central to who he was. Even if his family would have liked more space and a backyard, he knew that in the long run they'd all be worse off if he was miserable. Prioritizing himself in this way made him a better husband and a better father.

That lesson is just as true for mothers. As I saw with my own mom and as I see today with Benís, a happy mother is a good mother.

It's healthy to take care of yourself and your own needs sometimes in order to improve the quality of life of those you love. All parents make sacrifices for their children, but making sacrifices is not a good thing in itself—the goal is to do what it takes to provide a good life for your family and yourself.

In parenting, as in life, when trade-offs come at too high of a cost, they're actually not worth it.

This reminds me of something I learned one summer in high

school while hiking deep in the wilderness and carrying all of our supplies on our backs, with the National Outdoor Leadership School. They called it the first rule of emergency medicine: *don't create a second patient.* Make sure to keep yourself safe while you're treating someone who is injured or sick, or you won't be able to help them and someone else will have to help you.

While running a fast-growing company, trying to be a good husband and son, and raising three children, I take those lessons very seriously. Even though I have enough work responsibilities to keep me busy twenty-four hours a day and would love to spend *another* twenty-four hours each day with my family, I still find a way to make a little time for myself.

I love to watch movies with Benís after the kids are asleep even though it feels almost gluttonous to do so with life being so full. But this lets my mind wander in a way that leaves me feeling refreshed.

I've always been a runner, and I always feel great after I exercise whether I'm jogging by myself through the city or hopping on my Peloton bike at home.

After years of often working late into the night, I now make sure to get at least six hours of sleep every night even though there's always more to do.

As a parent, I've learned that focused play with my kids — tuning out my work and my other grown-up concerns for a while to just *be* with them — can sometimes count as "me time," too.

Finding time for myself is harder now than it used to be, of course. But it's still just as important. And I notice that when I don't I cannot be my best at work or home. I become less patient, make worse decisions, and feel constantly distracted. Letting myself get to that state isn't good, and taking care of myself helps everyone around me.

I couldn't *find* my place in the world — I had to *create* it
My failed search for professional belonging

Throughout my twenties, I was searching for not just a job and a career I could excel at — but a company that provided a sense of real community and belonging. But no matter how hard I tried, I continued to feel like an outsider, always out of place.

Sometimes, the places I worked did things that made me feel unwelcome. I was almost always the only Black person working on a team, often one of the only Black people working on an entire floor of a building. Even though I had attended an exclusive private high school and an Ivy League college, the shared references and generations-old social connections among my mostly White colleagues often eluded me.

There were the small comments that stung: the times people confused me with other Black people, the times people assumed I worked in the mail room, the awkward jokes about the racial comedy skits of Dave Chappelle's show, the people who said they were uncomfortable in Black neighborhoods, the many people who told me I was their first Black friend.

I could go on and on.

When I once asked why a company that was heavily investing in recruiting women didn't do the same to recruit and retain Black employees, I was told, "We tried so hard, but we didn't get the return on investment that we do with women."

Just imagine. How worthwhile would you feel if someone told you that people like you were simply not worth investing in? Would you feel like you'd found a company that could be your home and make you feel like you are part of the company family?

At other times, I blame myself for the distance I felt. Hungry for connection, I may have tried too hard to fit in. I'd learned how to act by watching how others acted and by paying careful attention to how people reacted to me, and that way of understanding the world helped me grow and learn and adapt quickly in so many ways. But it had come at a cost. I'd spent less time asking myself who I really was and more time asking what other people wanted me to be.

So when I saw one of my bosses start buying Ferragamo ties and noticed that some of my colleagues had started wearing them soon after, I didn't ask myself if I liked the style of those neckties or if they represented who I truly was. I just went out and bought a few, hoping that those ties would help me fit in, too.

The same thing happened when the CEO of Goldman Sachs bought a Timex Ironman watch. Without a second thought, I went to the store and bought one for $40 and put my Cartier and my Rolex (which I had purchased previously in order to fit in at other jobs) in my drawer. To this day, I've never worn either of them again.

Looking back, I hardly recognize the person who did those things. And that's no coincidence. I was actually *not being myself.* I was trying to blend in, trying to belong—and I was willing to act how I thought people wanted me to if it'd helped me get there.

As we all know, that approach never works. You never end up feeling like you belong if you're hiding who you truly are in the process.

When I started Compass with Ori, an Israeli immigrant, we set out to make Compass a place where anyone and everyone could belong.

I cannot speak for all 20,000 people in the Compass community of agents and employees, but for me, it has lived up to that promise. For the first time in my life, I feel like I'm able to show up at work as my full and authentic self.

I dress how I like — and see others throughout the company doing the same. Our offices in Malibu, California, and Montauk, New York, are filled with people who have prominent tattoos and go surfing regularly around their work schedule. In other markets, you'll see a lot of pearls, or cowboy boots, or preppy business casual, or hoodies-and-jeans start-up chic — often in the same office.

We have affinity groups that give people who share part of their identity a place to gather. We have put up Belonging Walls in offices on which people post stories of times when they've felt out of place and times they've felt exceptionally accepted.

But we didn't stop at that level of identity and community. We've built this mindset into the actual performance culture of the company. Rather than expecting everyone to be good at everything, we expect everyone to be *great* at some things and not so great at others, and to collaborate with one another in ways that maximize everyone's strengths while mitigating everyone's weaknesses.

Our mission is to help everyone find their place in the world, and that extends to our agents, our employees, and me. We want everyone to feel like this company is their place in the world. The type of professional home I could never find earlier in my journey. Somewhere where everyone belongs.

8

BOUNCE BACK WITH PASSION

It ain't about how hard you hit, it's about how hard you can *get* hit and still keep moving forward.

—Rocky Balboa

A champion is defined not by their wins but by how they recover when they fall.

—Serena Williams

Our greatest weakness lies in giving up. The most certain way to succeed is always to try just one more time.

—Thomas Edison

For everyone with a dream, there are countless doubters, skeptics, cynics, and competitors. For every impressive victory, there are many more crushing failures and defeats. For every great run of luck, there's the day when your luck runs out.

The truest test of character is not how you act when things are going great — it's what you do when you hit bottom.

Never stay down. Find the resilience to jump back up and stand even taller than before. Show your grit by continuing to push even when every fiber of your being is telling you to give up, quit, rest. Use your passion to keep dreaming big no matter how many times your dreams are dashed.

Resilience, grit, and passion are the difference between an entrepreneur and somebody who had a big idea once.

Resilience, grit, and passion are the difference between someone who's living their dreams and someone who's living with regret.

Think about it: when you're knocked flat on your back, there's literally nowhere to go but up. You can see with your own two eyes that the sky's the limit. The only thing left to do is to bounce back with passion *by returning to the beginning and dreaming big again.*

When you get knocked down, create a new dream to get back up for

How I lost a million dollars and then, in a single day, began to bounce back

The year 2000 was one of the hardest years of my life. And that was *before* I lost my entire life savings.

I was doing poorly at work. I felt like a fraud and knew that I wasn't likely to be rehired after my initial two-year stint. I could tell that I wasn't only in the wrong job — I was also in the wrong *profession*.

But let me back up a little.

From a young age, I'd learned how to make and save money. By the time I was a year out of college, I'd managed to sock away about $100,000, with the majority of that being money I'd earned (plus years of compound interest) running my high school DJ business.

The dot-com bubble was still growing and I decided to invest all of my savings in Internet stocks. What's more, I made the very dangerous choice to take on a margin loan so I could buy even more stocks. The margin loan allows you to magnify your upside if your stocks gain value, but it also magnifies your losses if the market goes down. (You may be able to see where this story is going.)

In a relatively short amount of time, I turned $100,000 in savings into almost $1 million. A million dollars! I felt like I was walking on air. I actually thought I was going to be able to retire right then and there. And then, as would happen if you *actually* tried to walk on air, I came crashing down to earth. My stocks started to fall in value. Just one or two at first, and by just a little. Then *all* of them by *a lot*. The crash picked up speed until my entire portfolio was worthless. It literally went to zero — and if I remember correctly, I think I even ended up owing the brokerages money.

From $100,000 to $1 million to less than zero.

My body knew things were bad before my brain did. Staring at the computer screen, my breath was short and shallow. My eyes didn't seem to want to focus. My hands were shaking.

For a long time that day, I did nothing at all. Didn't eat. Didn't move. But I finally picked up my phone, forced myself to remember how to make a call, and reached out to my mom.

It was hard to form words and sentences much less explain what had happened. But as soon as she made sense of what I was trying to say, she did what she always does when I'm in need: she flew into action. She found a therapist and got her to agree to see me that afternoon.

The therapist prescribed me a sedative so I could get some rest. When I got home, I took a pill and fell asleep. The next day, I woke up, and although I was still reeling, I wasn't in the state of shock I had been the day before. My brain replaced the devastating sense of loss with an energizing vision of the future. I began to take stock of my life and imagine how I could create a new and exciting future. After I'd spent a little time grounding myself in my new reality, I started to dream about the next five to ten years of my life.

I dreamed about applying to business school as a way to hit reset.

I dreamed about transitioning from consulting to investment banking to earn more money.

I dreamed about spending some time in the public sector after rebuilding my savings by working a few years on Wall Street.

I dreamed of starting a nonprofit as a way to give back to the community as soon as I was back on my feet myself.

Then I began charting out the path between where I was and where I wanted to be. I wrote out a six-month plan, two-year plan, and five-year plan.

The first step was business school, a way to start over professionally. As with most big decisions, I learned from people around me I respected. I saw that smart people were going to business school, so I decided to go to business school. Looking back, I'm surprised I decided to take on a huge amount of new student debt right after losing all of my savings, but learning from the wisdom of others gave me confidence.

I started researching the best schools, working backward from their application deadlines, reaching out to mentors for letters of recommendation, writing essays. I found that having a new dream to work toward gave me all the energy I needed to bounce back with passion.

That's the advantage of hitting rock bottom: you suddenly realize you have to change your outlook or you'll be stuck looking straight at the dirt on the ground. But if you can find a way to shift your eyes upward, you can see the blue of the sky once again. If you can dream a new dream when you're at your lowest, you will see there's nowhere to go but up.

Sometimes it takes a long time to bounce back
The breakup that almost broke me

I really thought I was going to marry Nicole.

We met at Columbia during my sophomore year. She was a year younger than I was, and I sought her out as soon as she arrived in New York because a friend of mine who'd known her in high school gave me an early heads-up that she was coming and was exactly the kind of girl I would fall for: a smart, charismatic, big dreamer who was also a Black and Jewish scholarship kid at a top private school. We got together her first semester and dated for the rest of college.

Our love was intense and energizing and complete. It felt like us against the world as we took on New York City as two lower-middle-class Black kids from the West Coast who weren't going to let anyone tell us what we couldn't do or stop us from achieving our dreams. We craved excellence. Early on in our relationship, I bought a copy of the Zagat restaurant guide, and we sought out the best of everything. The best twenty-four-hour restaurant. The best brunch. The best seafood. The best Italian. The best Japanese.

Nicole and I were keenly aware of how the world saw us — and how we wanted to be seen. For richer, Whiter, better-connected friends of ours, everything seemed so easy. I knew that other people weren't *better* than we were — but I wanted us both to be able to *feel* that, too. In an attempt to signify the status we deserved, I bought expensive watches for myself and expensive bracelets for her, but Nicole knew then what I learned soon after: that wasn't the answer.

For both of us, working twice as hard and refusing to put boundaries around our dreams was the answer.

We liked to have fun, but we spent the vast majority of our time together working. Studying and writing papers. Figuring out our futures. Planning the path between where we were and where we wanted to be. We both had big dreams, a high tolerance for hard work, and a strong desire to prove ourselves to the world, which is probably why we both graduated college in two and a half years.

I tried to convince Nicole to come work in management consulting after graduation like I was. But she made it very clear that this wasn't her dream. "I'm an artist, and I want to go to Hollywood," I believe she said, with a self-deprecating tone but very serious intention.

She was an actor, but we dreamed up a more powerful goal for her future: to run a major movie studio, which was nearly unheard of for a Black woman. Once she'd set her sights on that goal, we began working backward to find the shortest and quickest path to her future. What grad degrees would she need? What were the best internships and fellowships along the way? How could she make sure she got those? Who were the most powerful and well-respected producers in Hollywood and how could she work for them?

I didn't spend as much time studying in college as some students did, but I spent a lot of time preparing for interviews and meetings with mentors, and I helped Nicole do the same. We prepared for every eventuality. Who's going to be in the room? What should she say? What questions could she ask to crack open the opportunity further?

We were like chess players and mapmakers, thinking several moves ahead and charting our paths decades into the future.

When Nicole graduated, she decided to take a trip to Europe to visit her friends studying abroad before moving back to Los Angeles and chasing her dreams. She'd graduated after the fall semester, and I remember sitting down to watch a movie called *The Family Man* together that December before she left. In the first scene, Jack and Kate are at an airport where Jack is about to leave for an investment banking internship in London while Kate stays home for law school. Kate says she has a "bad feeling" about this and asks him to stay. She's worried that it will lead to their breaking up, and says, "The plan doesn't make us great. What we have together, that's what makes us great." But Jack goes to London for the internship. The next scene is many years later and you can see that their career ambitions led them to break up and have different lives. All this in the first three minutes of the movie.

Nicole and I both broke down crying. I think we both had a sense that we were at that exact same inflection point in our relationship. That we were both prepared to make sacrifices that would take us apart from each other. That things were never going to be the same.

The fact that we had seen it coming didn't make it any easier when it actually happened.

When Nicole returned from her trip to Europe, she'd decided that I wasn't part of her future anymore. She told me that she felt she had to go it alone. That she wanted the freedom and independence to explore her path to becoming a movie producer in LA and start the next chapter of her life on her own. That she wanted to be able to be young and make mistakes—and that it felt like neither of us had made a single mistake when we were together.

I. Was. Devastated.

After she broke up with me, I lost my mind. Every bad and obsessive trait I have came out in full force. I kept asking the same questions over and over and over again. How could someone who loves me decide to leave me? Why wouldn't she give me a chance to win her back? What can I do to get her back?

I tried everything I could think of for six months or more to get back together with Nicole, but nothing worked. I was a mess. I wasn't eating or sleeping or thinking straight. I lost more than twenty pounds.

In late summer of 2001, I flew out to LA to propose to her even though she'd given me absolutely no indication that she had any interest in me anymore. I somehow thought proposing to her was a good way to win her back. When I landed, I went to Tiffany's in Beverly Hills and bought a $26,000 engagement ring on my credit card.

I proposed that day and she said no. That night, with one final try, I drove to Nicole's house and held a boom box over my head playing our favorite song, just like John Cusack did in *Say Anything*. Eventually, her father came out and told me to leave. That was the moment I gave up, which ultimately was what I needed to do in order to move on. I went straight to the airport and booked the next flight home.

On the plane, I started to come to my senses. I realized that I had a lot of work to do on myself. When I got home, I began to get back into music, buying myself a guitar and trying to teach myself how to play. I made my first plan to start training for my first marathon.

The main thing I did, though, was work. For the next several years, there was *only* work in my life. My heart was as cold as ice.

The connection between Nicole and me had been built around shared ambition, striving, and progress. In the years that followed, I think I worked so hard for so long because deep down I was still trying to impress her. I thought that if I worked ridiculously hard and accomplished enough, she'd come back.

She never came back.

Instead, some years later, I ended up meeting the woman who actually *is* the love of my life. Nicole married someone wonderful, too. She and I are good friends now, and I'm so happy for the success and happiness we've both found in life, in different fields, and on different coasts. And as I always knew she would, she's accomplished her dream and is now president of a film division at a major Hollywood studio.

Looking back, I'm grateful to Nicole even though she broke my heart. I really don't know if I'd have the life I have now without the pain and devastation that came from our breakup. Just as our love propelled me through college and into my first job, the heartbreak I felt after our relationship crumbled sent me into professional overdrive for nearly half a decade at a crucial time in my life. The joy of being with Nicole helped me expand my dreams; the pain of living without her gave me the fuel to make them come true.

When I lost a million dollars in the stock market, I bounced back in a day. But when I lost her love, it took me more than *four years* to regain my footing. They included my final year at McKinsey, my entire business school experience, two years at Lazard, and a while after that. Being in pain for that long gave me an opportunity to focus and reflect that I wouldn't have found any other way. Like a training camp for an Olympic athlete, my relative solitude provided me time to work on myself and grow stronger.

It wasn't until I got to Washington, DC, as a White House Fellow that I started to see the other side of it. It's like when you get a deep cut that leaves a scab, and you look down and feel its rough edges day after day. Then one day you look down and it's gone.

That's how it felt in DC more than four years later. One day I sat down and wrote out more than one hundred goals for the rest of my life, some of which I shared earlier in this book. I was finally able to dream again.

When life throws you challenges and obstacles, sometimes you can deflect them and keep moving forward. Sometimes a setback knocks you clear off your feet and you need to dust yourself off and bounce back. And sometimes you get hit so hard that it takes years before you can start to see your future clearly again.

You can't start bouncing back until you realize you're off track

The simple way I discovered that we had to fundamentally change our strategy

The first year of Compass was a blur.

Before we even launched, we raised the largest seed round of venture capital funding in the country that year with the goal of revolutionizing apartment rentals in New York City.

I'd never run a company before, and I was learning so much each day from Ori, who had more experience than I did. We hired a team of brilliant software engineers as well as neighborhood specialists and booking coordinators to work with renters in New York. We began building technology and executing our strategy as quickly as possible. And we had a ton of fun along the way.

Everything was clicking. We were helping real customers find great apartments to rent. We had revenue coming in within eight months, which is rare for venture-funded start-ups. Enough of our metrics were going "up and to the right" that we were able to make pretty charts that got our investors excited about our growth.

Less than a year later, we raised a much larger Series A funding round.

It *felt* like we were succeeding. The team thought we were on the right track. After all, our investors had just demonstrated their confidence in us and our strategy with more funding.

There was just one problem: our model *wasn't actually working for our customers.*

As CEO of a very young start-up, I felt it was important to spend time working directly with our customers. So when I wasn't hiring, setting goals, or pitching investors, I always liked to get out of the office and work as a neighborhood specialist or a booking coordinator myself.

At that time, our neighborhood specialists were nice, smart people who generally hadn't worked in real estate before. We paid them on salary rather than on commission and outfitted them with a distinctive red backpack filled with items we thought the customer might want: breath mints, phone chargers, an umbrella, shoe polish. They'd meet people on a particular corner in a particular neighborhood and show them the best apartments in the area.

The booking coordinators would call up landlords to set up the tours beforehand. That was my first sign of trouble. When I was doing a shift as a booking coordinator, landlords kept asking me, "Who are you? Why should I talk to you?" The problem was that we had no relationships and no history. The landlords didn't trust us to deliver good renters, and our renters couldn't rely on us to help them steer clear of shady landlords.

Like many start-ups, we'd undervalued the importance of experience, knowledge, and relationships. But that wasn't the only problem.

When I was working as a neighborhood specialist one day, I met up with a client to show her apartments on the Lower East Side. I started out by asking her to tell me a little about herself and what she was looking for. "You're the third person I've had to say this to in the last twenty-four hours," she told me. She'd already checked out places in two other New York neighborhoods that weekend: Hell's Kitchen and Williamsburg—and she'd had to repeat the same explanation to a new neighborhood specialist every time!

Like many start-ups, we'd assumed that we understood the customer experience without spending enough time talking to and learning from customers. From our perspective, the way we'd set things up made a lot of sense—but it didn't make any sense at all to our customers. It was more streamlined for us and more inefficient for them.

What's more, I came to see how one of our major differentiators—providing rental advice without the incentives of commission-based sales—was actually leading to a worse experience for our customers.

Like many start-ups, we'd seen something we didn't like from the outside and opposed it without fully understanding the actual value it delivered.

In the last eight years of working with experienced real estate agents, I've been impressed with the wisdom, knowledge, connections, and care that commissioned real estate agents bring to each transaction. They have both a personal and an economic drive to deliver remarkable client service in order to build their reputation and generate referral business. It's an incentive that actually works out well for everyone involved.

One year in, the people on our team who spent their time in the office writing software and drawing exciting ideas on whiteboards thought we were doing great. But after I spent a day out in the field with our customers, it was easy to see that we were headed for disaster. We needed to change course quickly if we were going to survive. But most people in the company wanted to keep heading in the same direction.

I had underestimated how strongly attached people can get to a vision. Our team couldn't see what our customers saw and they couldn't hear what our customers were trying to tell us.

I sensed that we had a major problem. And I was determined to find a way to solve it.

What happened next, though—I did not see that coming at all.

Don't expect change to be easy
The secret breakfast I wasn't invited to

A few days after I started trying to persuade our leadership team to change course, Ori was invited to breakfast by a top company executive. When Ori arrived, he saw that every leader in the company was there—except me.

Ori sat. They talked. He listened. The team told Ori that they thought I was leading the company in the wrong direction. That I didn't get the big vision. That I had to go.

At that point, one year in, I was advocating for a fundamental strategic shift away from our neighborhood specialists toward experienced real estate agents, but the team wasn't buying it.

Ori told the team that he'd give it some thought and left. He called me up, invited me on a walk, and told me everything. I was shocked. My heart was racing, my stomach felt suddenly heavy, and my throat felt tight. For a little while, I didn't say anything at all.

I knew that starting and running a company would have its ups and downs, but I never once imagined that I'd be forced out by my own team.

Ori asked me to make the case once again for why I thought our big pivot was the right strategic choice. He said, "Let's go get cigars tonight." We had never smoked cigars before, but we'd talked about celebrating over cigars in the past. This wasn't exactly what I was expecting.

I went home to my apartment and talked to Benís. I shared what happened and how the team wanted me to leave. I shared my doubts and my insecurities. I told my wife that maybe I wasn't the right person for the job, that maybe I was taking the company in the wrong direction. She paused for a moment, looked me in the eyes, and said, "Bounce back, you've been through worse. You'll get through this, too." It was the first time I remember anyone saying "bounce back" to me.

When I met up with Ori that night, he asked me two questions. Over the years, I've been repeatedly impressed by how well he can get to the heart of a situation.

The first question: "Because of our backgrounds, we're going to continue to be able to raise money and hire talented people. And if we can mobilize our money and people to help agents be more successful, won't we be successful?"

I said yes with complete conviction.

The second question: "If you're being chased by a bear, you only need to be faster than the second person. If we change models, who is the second person?"

I said, "I think it would be a brokerage firm."

He said, "That'd be very good because brokerage firms don't move quickly." And definitely not as fast as our team was capable of moving.

In the face of an attempted coup by the team objecting to a change in direction, Ori had distilled the thesis of Compass with just two questions.

I knew Ori believed in me. And after that simple conversation, I knew we both believed in the company we were building and the direction I was leading it.

I said, "Let's do it." And every day since then, we've focused on helping agents be more successful, and we've moved faster than brokerage firms to create programs and tools to help agents grow their business and have a better quality of life.

I learned in my youth that when you're knocked down you need a dream to reach up for in order to bounce back. But I learned that day that when you're leading a team through a period of transformational change you need to help them *all* see the vision as clearly as you do. Before that secret breakfast, I'd underestimated how much work that would take.

When we invested in showing the entire team the potential that this new path unlocked, more than two-thirds of the staff decided to stay. Even though it was definitely a shocking and painful day, it helped us bounce back with passion and a sense of purpose that was clearer than it ever would have been if that breakfast hadn't happened.

Over time, it's become clearer and clearer that we made the

right call in that moment. Since our pivot, we've raised more than $1.5 billion in outside investment, hired more than 20,000 of the best real estate agents in the country, expanded to more than 150 markets, and built the most seamless and powerful real estate technology platform for agents in the industry. In the last three years, Compass agents have sold more than $200 billion in real estate and helped a quarter of a million people find their place in the world.

And it still feels like we're just getting started.

YOU'RE NOT
JUST HERE
FOR
YOURSELF

Belonging is worth fighting for

*The backlash against my underground newspaper, the wall
behind the theater, and the surprising power of mere words*

I was one of the very few kids of color in my elite private high
school. One day on the way home from school, Jibril, a friend of
mine who was a grade or two below me, told me the story of how
callously and thoughtlessly his teacher and his White classmates
were using the N-word in English class while discussing *Huckle-
berry Finn*. They used the word over and over, and when he raised
his hand to complain, the teacher dismissed his feelings. Feeling the need to defend my friend, I wrote up his experience as an
essay and submitted it to our school's newspaper, the *Uni Times*.

The newspaper rejected it. They said that my article was full
of fallacies. But how could it have been when it was merely sharing Jibril's emotional experience? They said it was a personal at-
tack on the teacher when it was meant as a call to understand

different points of view, especially between different levels of power and privilege.

It didn't stop there. Jibril and I were soon called into the teacher's office and intimidated into accepting her version of the facts.

As the weeks passed, our frustration grew and grew. Eventually, we decided that if the official student newspaper wouldn't print our stories we had to create our own — and *Contraband* was born. We put together a new underground newspaper featuring my essay along with several others from students whose voices hadn't been heard, made a bunch of copies, and distributed them for free throughout the school.

The response was swift and aggressive. The school administration came after us and our parents for the fact that we had photocopied the newsletter on the school's machines without permission. Rather than engage with the substance of our experience, they tried to silence us and criminalize us using a technicality. The controversy escalated. Meetings were called. People took sides. We printed additional letters to defend ourselves.

But in the end, their pushback largely worked. They divided the student body and the teachers. My mom and I, along with the other kids and their moms, got called out by the administration. I recently learned that during all of this the school's board of trustees met with the faculty and told them to hold their breath until we graduated and it all blew over.

Later that year, I remember a Black classmate of mine asking me if *Contraband* had been worth it. I told her that it hadn't been — and I really believed it. The whole thing had started with a student saying that he felt like he didn't belong and the experience only made it that much clearer just how much he and I actually did *not* belong, or feel comfortable, in that community. It felt like nothing changed.

A few years passed.

I came back to San Francisco from New York for a visit and caught up with a younger friend who'd been a freshman when I was a senior. I reminisced about what a difficult final year I'd had because of *Contraband*. And he looked at me, and said, "But you've seen the Wall, haven't you?"

I didn't know what he was talking about, so he took me there.

In a long back hallway behind the theater in my high school, something beautiful had emerged. A free speech wall, where you could write anything that you believed to be true. If you didn't feel heard or seen by the broader community, you now had a dedicated space where you could speak out. A vibrant conversation was happening with paint and markers, and I saw messages from kids of color who were still being discriminated against, White girls battling anorexia, unpopular kids who were proudly declaring their own existence and value. Every inch of the wall was full of uncensored, unfiltered free expression from students. It had even spread onto the ceiling.

"*Contraband* inspired us," my friend told me.

Standing in that hallway, I realized that we're not just here for ourselves, that our actions can have an impact that we can't predict and perhaps will never see. The loudest, most negative reactions are not the only ones that matter; in fact, the most important reactions are often unseen and unheard, and come from people who desperately needed to know they weren't alone.

The truth is, nearly everyone feels out of place and misunderstood — especially in high school but also throughout life. Everyone wants to feel known. Everyone wants to be able to be their full and authentic self. Everyone wants to belong.

I had taken a big risk with *Contraband*, paid a big price, and decided that it wasn't worth it. For years after high school, I'd hidden the outspoken part of myself, internalizing the lesson they had tried to teach me: that speaking my mind had too many consequences. But I was wrong.

In that hallway, I recommitted to speaking out when my voice could help others understand that they truly belong. I realized that words *can* have real power — at least for some people some of the time.

That's what drove me to create *Contraband* in the first place. And it's what drove me to write this book. My story may not mean much to some people. The lessons I've learned from mothers, mentors, and my years on this planet might not connect with everyone.

But for people who really need it — who need to see their story and their struggle reflected — I hope I've offered a bit of hope and comfort and a path forward from wherever you are to the place where you truly belong. You — yes, you — deserve to find your place in the world. I hope this book has helped make that feel just a little bit more possible.

ACKNOWLEDGMENTS

I hope this book has conveyed my deep conviction that whatever success I have achieved in life would not have been possible without the help of too many people to count.

The same is true of the book itself.

This project wouldn't have gotten off the ground if it weren't for Benís — my wife, my partner, my coach, my coparent, my inspiration, and my love. She saw the opportunity, felt the moment, pulled the team together, and helped me see her vision. Benís was my first reader and gave valuable feedback on every line in this book — all while also running her own business, raising our girls, bringing our son into the world, and helping our family navigate the pandemic.

I would not have had anything to write a book about, of course, without the advice, guidance, and generosity of the countless mentors who've inspired me along my journey. To those of you not directly quoted or named in the book, please know that any omissions were due to a lack of space, not a lack of wisdom or impact.

But it all started with one woman: my mom. I wouldn't have learned to dream big, move fast, learn from reality, be solutions driven, obsess about opportunity, collaborate without ego, maximize my strengths, or bounce back with passion if my mother, Ruth Reffkin, hadn't provided me with such an excellent example of entrepreneurialism from my very earliest days. I'm so grateful to you, Mom, for always being in my corner and I'm so proud of everything you've accomplished and all the lives you've touched.

I couldn't ask for a wiser business partner or a better friend than Ori Allon. If it wasn't for him, Compass would not exist.

I want to thank all the people who took time out of their busy lives to sit down for interviews as part of this process, including my godfather, Gene Reffkin; my mom's ex-boyfriend (and Gene's bandmate), Paul Dresher; my mother-in-law, Elida Reyes; my best friend (and earliest business partner) Jabali Sawicki; my fifth grade teacher, Julie Blank; my high school physics professor, Nasif Iskander; my business school tax professor, Robert Willens; my college girlfriend, Nicole; and my colleague, friend (and real estate legend) Leonard Steinberg.

I'd especially like to thank the Compass agents who have shared their entrepreneurial stories with me over the years. I've learned so much from each and every one of you.

I couldn't have completed the book, while running a 20,000-person company at the same time, without the help of my writing partner, Peter Koechley. For most of a year, we worked together nearly every Saturday night from 8 to 10 p.m. to turn my stories and the lessons I've learned into chapters. He exemplifies the principle of collaborating without ego. And he, like me, married a woman smarter than himself, Krista Williams, who offered insightful feedback on the entire manuscript.

Jim Levine and his team at Levine Greenberg Rostan taught me that literary agents are just as vital to the process of writing a book as real estate agents are to the process of selling a home. Jim didn't just help me find the right publisher, he helped me figure out what book I wanted to write.

As a lifelong believer in the power of education, I'm thrilled to be publishing with Houghton Mifflin Harcourt, led by Ellen Archer and Deb Brody. I'm grateful to my editor, Rick Wolff, and his editorial assistant, Olivia Bartz, who helped us shape the book and find the heart in each story; Heather Tamarkin, who oversaw the book's production; David Hough, who copyedited the manuscript and does not like the word "actually"; Denise Long, who checked my facts; Greta Sibley, who crafted the interior design; Chloe Foster, who oversaw the interior design; Brian Moore, who art directed the cover; and Lori Glazer, who saw this book's potential very early on. On the publicity side, I'd like to thank Michelle Triant and Mark Fortier for helping share the lessons that helped me so much in my life with so many more people.

Thanks to everyone Benís convened in the very early days to help chart the path for this book, namely Julie Binder, Matt Spangler, Jeff Hunter, and Rory Golod. And as always, I want to acknowledge my tremendous team at Compass: David O'Connell, my chief of staff; Anna Feagan, my executive communications lead; and Caitlin Jovovich and Carol Oliveira, who help make everything I do possible.

I'll end where the book begins: with a dedication to my children. I am and will forever be grateful to Raia, Ruby, and River for being perfect just as they are and for filling my life with lightness and hope. I wish you lives full of big dreams, larger purpose, and deep belonging.

INDEX

Index 227

Lee, Eduard Rodney. *See* Eduard
(father)
listening, 98–101, 142–45

marathons, 101–3, 159–61
marriage, 137–40
maximize your strengths (principle of entrepreneurship),
30–32, 61–63, 73–76,
109–11, 184–96
McGuire, Ray, 97, 187
McKinsey & Company, 43–47,
130, 189–90, 192
mentors
building relationships with,
90–94
college opportunities, 88–90
constructive feedback from,
36, 82–85
following in their footsteps,
101–3
networks, creating, 86–88
overview of, 81–82
principles of, 91–92
push towards achievement
from, 98–101
risk and, 103–5
unwritten rules, 85–86
mindfulness, 134–35
Moore, Wes, 123
Mornell, Linda, 83–85
mothers, as entrepreneurs

family and, 76–78
independence and, 54–58
overview of, 53–54
perseverance, 58–66
rediscovering oneself, 69–73
self-acceptance, 73–76
self-care, 192
motivation
to achieve dreams, 19, 44–45
accomplishments, historical,
154–55
finding and using, 159–61
forgiveness and, 26
inspiration and, 101–3
from people, 155–59
recruitment and, 177–79
move fast (principle of entrepreneurship), 40–43, 48–50,
64–66, 109–11, 124–35
movies, as inspiration, 114–17
multitasking, 129

National Foundation for Teaching Entrepreneurship,
23–24, 63
National Outdoor Leadership
School, 62, 83–85, 193
Network for Teaching Entrepreneurship, 23–24
networking
access to and privilege, 85–86
creating your own, 86–88